Being human – our identity – is argu[...] issues of our era. We are being call[...] stand biblically who we are: created, [...] restored. The answer has vast implications, from debates around the beginning and end of life to understanding human sexuality, from self-esteem and mental health through to how we raise our children.

Paul Mallard's book comes as an essential but highly accessible and readable contribution to a growing recovery of our doctrine of man. Mallard as a pastor understands that we need to be biblically relevant in our thinking, so guides us through Ephesians with the lens of human identity in a way that is truth-filled, devotional and grounded both in Scripture and in life.

**Dr Andrew Collins**, consultant psychiatrist and biblical counsellor

In this excellent and engaging book, Mallard leads his readers through Ephesians to explore important issues of identity and offers a beautiful and moving presentation of the gospel, as the truth that both saves us and shapes our lives as believers.

The mixture of stories from family life, ministry and university days, along with the way that he carefully unpacks Scripture and concludes each chapter with a set of questions for consideration and reflection, makes for a really interesting, encouraging and practical read that is sure to be exceptionally helpful in a culture so concerned with and confused by questions of identity and meaning.

**Ellie Cook**, staff worker with UCCF: The Christian Unions, blogger and speaker

In a culture unsettled and confused about questions of identity, Paul Mallard's rich and timely book calls his Christian readers to grasp and live the transformative power of knowing who God has made them to be. With theological depth and a pastor's heart, Paul paints a vivid picture of the God who loves us as his children in Christ, and who is restoring us to the glory for which we were made. The book brims with hope and confidence, and it fills the reader with a sense of the immeasurable worth of being in Christ. That a book about human identity ultimately lifts our eyes to worship and adore the God in whom we find that identity is perhaps the book's greatest recommendation. I pray that Christians of all ages will read it, let its truth soak in and then live life in the joyful confidence of who they are in Christ.

**Richard Cunningham**, Director of UCCF: The Christian Unions

An invaluable and accessible resource that will take young believers a long way towards being anchored in the kind of Christian faith which can withstand the turmoil and chaos of life.

Maturity in our Christian life is directly proportional to the rootedness and depth of our grasp of our identity in Christ. So many pastoral problems and difficulties originate in a lack of understanding of something that Jesus has already given us – a new identity. So much stability and growth occur when this objective reality is grasped, applied, treasured and remembered.

Church leaders and all involved in ministry with teenagers and students will benefit enormously from reading this book, and from its extremely helpful discussion questions. The author has provided us with gospel realism that will bring stability and understanding to many Christians currently at sea – and only because of a lack of a true understanding of what the Lord Jesus has done for us and given to us.

**Peter Dickson**, Regional Team Leader for Scotland, UCCF: The Christian Unions

Paul writes with the gentleness of one who has known suffering. He includes quotes from others that bring you into a community. He lets Scripture invite us and shape us. I thought I was walking through the English countryside with a wise friend.

**Dr Ed Welch**, counsellor and faculty member, Christian Counseling and Educational Foundation

# AN IDENTITY
# TO DIE FOR

Know who you are

Paul Mallard

INTER-VARSITY PRESS
36 Causton Street, London SW1P 4ST, England
Email: ivp@ivpbooks.com
Website: www.ivpbooks.com

*First published 2020*

**British Library Cataloguing-in-Publication Data**
A catalogue record for this book is available from the British Library.

ISBN: 978–1–78359–938–7
eBook ISBN: 978–1–78359–939–4

Set in Minion Pro 11/14pt
Typeset in Great Britain by CRB Associates, Potterhanworth, Lincolnshire
Printed in Great Britain by Ashford Colour Press Ltd, Gosport, Hampshire

*Inter-Varsity Press publishes Christian books that are true to the Bible and that
communicate the gospel, develop discipleship and strengthen the church for its mission
in the world.*

*IVP originated within the Inter-Varsity Fellowship, now the Universities and Colleges
Christian Fellowship, a student movement connecting Christian Unions in universities
and colleges throughout Great Britain, and a member movement of the International
Fellowship of Evangelical Students. Website: www.uccf.org.uk. That historic association
is maintained, and all senior IVP staff and committee members subscribe to the
UCCF Basis of Faith.*

Dedicated to Abe – the 'golden prince'
who inspired me to write this book

# Contents

# Contents

# Preface

Abraham Kirk Arthur Morgan invaded our lives on 19 September 2018.

I had arrived home from a church meeting and Edrie, my wife, greeted me with a poorly repressed grin.

'You need to ring your daughter,' she informed me.

Keziah sounded tired but elated.

'I'm OK, Dad, and so is the baby. He even has a shock of blond hair.'

Within days we visited and instantly fell in love with our newest grandchild – how could anyone not? Everything seemed normal and, with the prejudice allowed to grandads, I decided that Abe was one of the most outstanding babies I had ever seen.

But then another phone call changed everything.

Abe had been admitted to hospital with seizures. For weeks the neurologists struggled to arrive at a diagnosis. After a series of tests and the numbing pain and agony of waiting, his parents learned that Abe was suffering from a set of rare brain disorders called lissencephaly.

I had never heard of this and my daughter even had to spell it for us – my grandson was the victim of a condition that I couldn't even spell. Literally, lissencephaly means 'smooth brain', a rare set of disorders and malformation characterized by the absence of normal folds in the cerebral cortex. In practice, Abe will probably never walk or talk or recognize his parents. Further tests went on to reveal that he also had very limited vision.

Edrie and I visited soon after the news broke. We tried to bring words of comfort, but at such times the reassurance of unconditional love is probably the best gift of all. As we prepared to leave at the end of our visit, Edrie hugged Keziah and together they sobbed, shedding tears more eloquent than words.

Fast-forward a few months and Abe was able to return home from hospital. We gathered as family and friends to celebrate his life and to thank God for him. I spoke briefly from Psalm 139:

> For you created my inmost being;
>> you knit me together in my mother's womb.
>
> I praise you because I am fearfully and wonderfully made;
>> your works are wonderful,
>> I know that full well.
>
> My frame was not hidden from you
>> when I was made in the secret place,
>> when I was woven together in the depths of the earth.
>
> Your eyes saw my unformed body;
>> all the days ordained for me were written in your book
>> before one of them came to be.
>
> How precious to me are your thoughts, God!
>> How vast is the sum of them!
>
> (Psalm 139:13–17)

We know that Abe is no accident or miscalculation on the part of a distant deity. Rather, he is fearfully and wonderfully made by a loving and kind Creator who wove him together in the secret place. David's psalm celebrates the uniqueness that every human being possesses. We know a lot today about cell division and genes and inherited characteristics, but we can also affirm that God forms each one of us, creating us with a special set of capacities and amazing potential. In spite of all his disabilities, Abe is a unique and valuable human being, made in the image of God; a little boy, but with immeasurable dignity.

It was meeting Abe that made me want to write this book about identity.

In people's eyes, Abe's limited quality of life might suggest a lack of value. Our real identity, however, is not related to our potential, nor is our dignity based on our 'value to society'. Whatever my gender, race, age, intellectual capacity or social standing, I enjoy a unique value and identity arising from the very fact that God made me in his own image.

This is true for all of us, but the Bible takes it further: 'In him we have redemption through his blood, the forgiveness of sins, in accordance with the riches of God's grace that he lavished on us' (Ephesians 1:7).

Christ died on the cross in order to forgive my sins and to make all things new. His death changed everything.

If I am a Christian, then I not only have the dignity of being made in the image of God but also being in Christ makes my identity even more glorious. Once, I was God's enemy, but now I have been redeemed, forgiven, reconciled and brought into his family. God has loved me with an everlasting love that will never ever fail. One day he will restore everything that sin and a damaged world have robbed me of.

What amazing irony! Because the sinless Jesus died in our place, we can have a whole new identity, one that we could never deserve or earn by our own efforts or merits. Through his death, we enjoy the best identity imaginable. It's (literally) an identity to die for. The irony doesn't end there, because daily, as we live for Christ, for us, dying becomes part of our new identity.

We'll start by looking at who we are, followed by an exploration of the subject in four parts. Come, journey with me and discover who you are – who you *really* are!

# Acknowledgments

I want to thank all those whose helpful suggestions have shaped this book: Thomas Brewer, Marjie Hutchinson, Hilary and Howard Jackson, Susannah Padiachy and Eleanor Trotter.

I also want to thank the congregation at Widcombe Baptist Church, Bath. I love you and I love serving you.

I want to thank Matthew and Keziah, Avennah and Genie for the example they have set in their bravery and passionate devotion to Abe, a very special little boy.

Finally, I want to thank Edrie, who is a constant source of joy and inspiration.

# 1
# Who am I?

## Hot crumpets and odd encounters

One cold winter's day in November 1973, I boarded a train at New Street Station, Birmingham. The following day I was due to attend an interview that would determine whether or not I would obtain a place to read theology at Selwyn College, Cambridge.

I felt very apprehensive.

I grew up in a working-class family in Birmingham. My dad was employed in a grocery shop and also did night shifts at Cadbury's chocolate factory. Mum did a variety of jobs that gave us the few luxuries we enjoyed. No one in my family had ever taken A levels before, never mind gone to university. The idea of going to Cambridge seemed beyond the bounds of imagination. My gran warned me about the dangers of forgetting my roots. Ivory towers seemed a million miles away from anything I had ever experienced.

My school had arranged for me to meet up with an ex-pupil in the second year of a natural sciences degree, so I located his room and we spent the evening toasting crumpets in front of a two-bar electric fire.

I began to relax.

Maybe Cambridge wouldn't be such an exotic place after all. Perhaps the ivory towers were not so different from the down-to-earth realities of Birmingham.

Then in came Tony.

He didn't knock, but just walked in and sat cross-legged on the floor between my host and me. He didn't say a word, nor did he acknowledge us. Yet my host kept on talking to me as if this was the most natural thing in the world.

The crumpets warmed up and we began to eat. I took one. So did Tony. Still not a word. I took a second and Tony followed suit. This went on until the plate was empty. At this point, still without speaking, Tony got up and walked out into the night.

I must have looked fairly mystified, but my host merely smiled and confided, 'That's Tony. He's in his second year studying philosophy, and he's not sure whether he exists or not.'

For someone who doubted the reality of his existence, he wasn't bad at polishing off crumpets!

## The importance of identity and self-worth

I learned some years later that Tony had become an accountant, so there was light at the end of this particular philosophical tunnel.

I suppose that few of us share Tony's existential dilemma. Most of us, however, wrestle with 'big' questions from time to time. In particular, we grapple with the plethora of questions surrounding the issue of identity and self-image.

- Who am I?
- How do I see myself?
- How do others see me?
- What does God think about me?

Such questions impinge on the even more personal anxieties associated with self-worth.

- Do I feel valued?
- Do I have significance?
- Could anyone really love me?

We live in a culture that is obsessed with these kinds of questions.

In some ways, we affirm the importance of a healthy self-image. We want to feel good about ourselves and the advertising industry takes full advantage of this. Getting a faster car, a better smartphone or the latest technological device will help me build up a positive self-image. At the very least, it can make me feel superior to someone else.

The greatest danger to personal and social health, we are assured, is a low self-image. This, rather than the love of money, is the root of all kinds of evil. Make people feel good about themselves and you will heal all the ills of society. A poor self-image may lead to depression, loss of potential and a willingness to tolerate abusive situations and relationships.

One social critic expresses it like this:

> incantations for self-worth, self-love and self-acceptance ooze out of the TV tube, drift across the radio waves, and entice through advertising. From the cradle to the grave, self-promoters promise to cure all of society's ills through doses of self-esteem, self-worth, self-acceptance, and self-love. And everyone or nearly everyone echoes the refrain: 'You just need to love and accept yourself the way you are.'[1]

Self-esteem and self-love have never been so important or prominent.

## The crisis of identity

In other ways, however, we have never been as unsure of our identity as we are today.

If the new atheists are to be believed, we humans are nothing more than machines made out of meat, whose only purpose is to perpetuate our genes. Why? To continue the species. Why? The answer is not clear. If matter is all that there is, can we really have any purpose or significance? If not, then where does that leave us?

Richard Dawkins insists that the universe is governed by blind forces with no design or purpose, no right or wrong. Seeking an ultimate meaning is a pointless exercise in self-deception.[2]

Of course, others have struggled with this too. The main character in Woody Allen's film, *Midnight in Paris*, is an aspiring writer who goes back in time to encounter famous authors from the past. One of these, Gertrude Stein, encourages him, as an artist, to provide a life-affirming alternative to what she describes as the inherent hopelessness of human existence.

Is it not desirable, then, to simply give up any search for ultimate purpose and make the most of what we have?

In the words of French philosopher and author Albert Camus, 'You will never be happy if you continue to search for what happiness consists of. You will never live if you are looking for the meaning of life.'[3]

The author of the book of Ecclesiastes[4] was well aware of this existential angst millennia ago. Imagining a world where only material things exist – a world 'under the sun' – he comes to a devastating conclusion:

'Meaningless! Meaningless!'
   says the Teacher.
'Utterly meaningless!
   Everything is meaningless.'
(Ecclesiastes 1:2)

It is clear that writers and artists have struggled with identity issues for centuries.

## Looking in the right place

The important issue is not that we get an elevated self-image, but that we get an accurate self-image.

Where do we look for this? We could look into the mirror of popular opinion and be shaped by what people say. This is a very tempting solution. Few of us are immune to the judgment of others. We want people to think that we are cool, successful, clever or beautiful. We allow a cacophony of voices to shape our identity. The problem is that these voices vary so much in their assessments. We can easily end up becoming people pleasers, constantly changing our image, chameleon-like, depending on our environment. But do we really want to go through our whole life wearing a series of uncomfortable and ill-fitting masks?

If we are brave, we may, instead, look into ourselves and seek to define our identity by what we see there. Forget what people say. I will be true to myself. I will never wear a mask. People must take me as they find me.

Now, this sounds wonderfully liberating but it has two drawbacks. First, we are social creatures and our identity is shaped by our relationships. It is very difficult to cut ourselves off from other people. Refusing to listen to what others say about us can result in eccentricity and isolation. Ploughing my own furrow might lead me into some very strange and lonely fields. Second, how honest can I really be about myself? Self-knowledge is elusive. My vision is subjective and skewed.

The mirrors of popular opinion and personal reflection prove to be distorted and distorting.

Is there a third option?

In the Bible, God – who made us and knows us best – has given us a definitive and perfect reflection of our identity. The Bible is God's accurate and unerring account of the true origin, nature and identity of human beings. This is the mirror into which we must look if we are truly to know ourselves and what we are meant to be.

However, this mirror is designed to not only inform but also to transform. If we merely look into the mirror and then walk away, it will never yield its treasures to us.

Do not merely listen to the word, and so deceive yourselves. Do what it says. Anyone who listens to the word but does not do what it says is like someone who looks at his face in a mirror and, after looking at himself, goes away and immediately forgets what he looks like. But whoever looks intently into the perfect law that gives freedom and continues in it – not forgetting what they have heard, but doing it – they will be blessed in what they do.
(James 1:22–25)

When we look into this mirror, what does it show us? We see that:

- God made us;
- sin marred us;
- grace transforms us.

## God made us to have humble dignity

The first thing that the mirror reflects back is the humble dignity and worth of all human beings. Our race is not the random product of time, matter and chance. We were created by a special act of God and are designed in a particular way and for a specific purpose.

> Then God said, 'Let us make mankind in our image, in our likeness, so that they may rule over the fish in the sea and the birds in the sky, over the livestock and all the wild animals and over all the creatures that move along the ground.'
> (Genesis 1:26)

We human beings are finite and personal. As finite creatures, we depend on God for every breath in our bodies. As personal beings we have the unique dignity of bearing his image and likeness, as we saw earlier.

What do we mean by the image of God? We show this in many ways:

- we are personal beings capable of relationships, language, reasoned thought and creativity;
- we are moral beings, responsible for the consequences of our actions;
- we are purposeful beings, created to serve God as vice-regents, responsibly ruling over his creation on his behalf; we are the real 'guardians of the galaxy'.

The Bible tells me that my identity should be expressed in terms of the relationships that God has established. I relate to him as my Creator and Sovereign Lord. I relate to other humans as equal image-bearers and partners. I relate to the world as the sphere in which I fulfil my God-given destiny.

## Meeting Esme

My eldest granddaughter, Esme, is eleven at the time of writing. We met her on the day after her birth. I well remember the wonder of holding her in my arms for the first time.

Becoming a granddad was a brand-new experience. What was totally unexpected was the sense of awe that I felt. I had been there at the birth of my own children and remember the wonder that it brought, but this was somehow different. Bringing up children is as tough as it is rewarding. When you meet your children's children there is a different kind of emotion, which is difficult to define. There is a sense of continuity – a feeling of a circle being completed. What's more, grandchildren are such fun! You don't have to worry about rules and routines – you can leave that to their parents.

No wonder Solomon tells us, 'Children's children are a crown to the aged' (Proverbs 17:6).

As I held that little bundle of life in my arms for the first time, my mind went to Psalm 8:

When I consider your heavens,
    the work of your fingers,
the moon and the stars,
    which you have set in place,
what is mankind that you are mindful of them,
    human beings that you care for them?
You have made them a little lower than the angels
    and crowned them with glory and honour.
You made them rulers over the works of your hands;
    you put everything under their feet.
(Psalm 8:3–6)

Irrespective of class, culture or competence, every person bears the image of God.

Meeting Esme, like meeting my grandson Abe, taught me that everyone we meet is a matchless creation, with immeasurable worth.

# Sin marred us – we are ruined masterpieces

Scripture's mirror reveals a second truth.

Sin has significantly defaced God's image. It has poisoned my relationships and affected the orientation of my heart, so that now I am self-centred rather than God-centred.

We constantly try to downplay sin and its consequences, but the mirror of Scripture won't let us get away with that. Sin is an act of violent rebellion against God, resulting in the corruption of the heart and the defacing of the image.

Listen to the Baptist minister C. H. Spurgeon:[5]

> Sin is a defiance of God to his face, a stabbing of God, so far as man can do it, to the very heart! Sin is a monster, a hideous thing, a thing which God will not look upon, and which pure eyes cannot behold but with the utmost detestation. A flood of tears is the proper medium through which a Christian should look at sin.

John Bunyan, author of *The Pilgrim's Progress*, says that sin is 'the dare of God's justice, the rape of his mercy, the jeer of his patience, the slight of his power, the contempt of his love'![6]

Sin is always personal. It is the fist that strikes the face of Christ. Sin turns me in on myself and promotes the kind of self-love that corrupts my mind and will and emotions. I do sinful things because I have a sinful heart. The spring is corrupted – no wonder the water is bitter. Jesus says:

> What comes out of a person is what defiles them. For it is from within, out of a person's heart, that evil thoughts come – sexual immorality, theft, murder, adultery, greed, malice, deceit, lewdness, envy, slander, arrogance and folly. All these evils come from inside and defile a person.
> (Mark 7:20–23)

We were created as God's masterpiece, but we have been defaced by sin. We have been ruined.

## Witley Court

Have you ever visited Witley Court? It is a ruin of an Italianate mansion in Worcestershire, built in the seventeenth century and expanded in the nineteenth by the architect John Nash. In 1937, a fire devastated the building and it has never been restored. Stand amid the ruins and you will see the degradation, but look carefully and you can appreciate what it once was. Shut your eyes and you can imagine the beauty that once resided there. It is a ruin, but a spectacular ruin!

We are similarly ruined masterpieces.

We feel the cold clutch of decay in everything we do. We are conscious that even when we do our best, it is affected by the baleful influence of self. At the same time, we know that there is more to us than this. Something is missing; something is broken. We long for what we cannot always define.

I am a sinner, but I have dignity because I still bear God's image. The preacher who wants to pander to my sense of self-worth, telling me that the most important thing in life is that I learn to love myself, is doing me a disservice. So too is the one who tells me that I am worthless.

Look at the way in which Jesus treated people. He was not afraid to expose hypocrisy and never pulled his punches when it came to confronting sin. In fact, he took the definition of sin deeper than anyone else, uncovering the roots of rebellion in the human heart. At the same time, when meeting with people in need, there was never a snide word or an unkind gesture. He welcomed sinners and restored renegades.

## Healthy self-suspicion

Reading the Bible should alert us to the dangers of the unhealthy self-love that belongs to the culture of self-esteem of our day. It is clear from the Bible that we are called to love God with all our heart and soul, with our strength and mind, and to love our neighbour. But we are not called to love ourselves. Indeed, the Bible consistently tells us to do just the opposite.

With his eyes on the cross, Jesus commands his disciples:

Whoever wants to be my disciple must deny themselves and take up their cross and follow me. For whoever wants to save their life will lose it, but whoever loses their life for me will find it.
(Matthew 16:24–25)

Denying the self is saying 'no' to selfish desires and longing for personal comfort. The word 'deny' is used elsewhere to describe Peter's vehement denial of Jesus. We are to be equally vehement in saying no to our own sinful cravings. Taking up the cross meant only one thing in the first century – the cross-carrier was a dead man walking. We are to follow Jesus to the place where sacrifice leads to the death of selfish desires and sinful ambitions.

This is a healthy antidote to the kind of thinking that promotes self-esteem as the ultimate virtue and self-denial as a dangerous and damaging aberration.

It also leads us to the third thing that the mirror of Scripture reveals to us.

## Grace transforms us

God's purpose is to restore the image that has been so badly defaced. Christ's work is one of glorious renovation. The Holy Spirit's agenda is to recreate the image of God in us. This process is at work in those who have put their faith in Christ.

As Paul puts it, 'For those God foreknew he also predestined to be conformed to the image of his Son, that he might be the firstborn among many brothers and sisters' (Romans 8:29).

The Bible tells the greatest story ever: God's plan to rescue and restore broken people. To do this, God takes on their identity. He becomes one of them and absorbs within himself the consequences of their rebellion. When he breaks out of the prison of death, he rescues the human race from the destruction they rightfully deserve. His mission is accomplished and applied to all who put their trust in him. As a Christian, I am a new creation being prepared for a new creation. All that I am now is defined by my relationship with God.

This is what Paul means when he says that we are 'in Christ', a phrase that holds the key to unlocking the treasure house of Christian identity. All the blessings of God come to us through Christ. God blesses Christ and then unites us to him and grants the same blessings to us. It does not depend on our performance, feelings or circumstances. Once we are 'in Christ', we are in him for ever.

When a poor woman marries a rich man, the two are legally joined and all his riches become hers. We have been joined to Christ. All his treasures have become ours.

The purpose of this book is to explore some of the treasures of our new identity. These far surpass anything that we could ever imagine. If we fail to get excited by them, then it is only because we have not understood them.

Jesus died to give us this amazing identity. It is an identity to die for. Literally.

## Getting to know Ephesians

On our journey, there are many places in the Bible to which we could turn, but I have deliberately chosen Paul's letter to the church in Ephesus.

When Christians write on the subject of identity, they tend to follow one of two paths. One popular approach is to explore the Bible's teaching from creation to the fall, and on to redemption and new creation. Another approach is to look at the various words and metaphors that are used to describe our identity – saint, sheep, son, soldier and so on.

Both methods are useful and good, but I have chosen a slightly different path. We will explore the theme by looking at a series of passages in the book of Ephesians, not covering every part, but allowing its flow to direct us. It's a bit like expository preaching: the

Bible passage rather than the preacher sets the agenda. I will cover the usual bases, but we may also find ourselves in some unexpected places!

Ephesians is one of the most comprehensive statements of the Christian faith ever penned. Ephesus itself was the capital of the Roman province of Asia Minor, a wealthy, religious and self-confident city, dominated by the temple of Diana and steeped in witchcraft. It was intellectually proud and morally corrupt. Paul planted a church there and stayed for three years (Acts 19:1–22). It became a hub church that, in turn, planted other churches.

Paul's letter to the Ephesians was written to strengthen and encourage Gentile Christians living at the heart of a pagan society. The first part of the letter (Ephesians 1 – 3) describes the riches of God's grace given to us in Christ. In the second part (Ephesians 4 – 6), Paul explains how this knowledge affects every part of our lives – the church, the world and the home.

Paul takes the dire consequences of sin very seriously. He describes the human condition in lurid terms: 'All of us also lived among them at one time, gratifying the cravings of our flesh and following its desires and thoughts. Like the rest, we were by nature deserving of wrath' (Ephesians 2:3).

Yet, because of God's grace, we have been reconciled to him, and he is in the process of transforming us into the likeness of Christ. One day this will be completed and Jesus will reign with a new humanity over a restored creation:

With all wisdom and understanding, he made known to us
the mystery of his will according to his good pleasure, which
he purposed in Christ, to be put into effect when the times
reach their fulfilment – to bring unity to all things in heaven
and on earth under Christ.
(Ephesians 1:8–10)

Ephesians, therefore, is an ideal place to search for spiritual wisdom.

# The restoration of the masterpiece

Back in November 1973, following my interview, I was offered a place to read theology at Cambridge. I began my studies the following October.

Each day, I walked through the grounds of King's College to reach the theology faculty building. Perhaps the most iconic image of Cambridge is the view across the River Cam with King's College Chapel in the background.

The chapel is magnificent. It is probably the finest example of late Perpendicular Gothic architecture in England. For many people, Christmas begins at 3 p.m. on Christmas Eve, when the voice of a lone chorister heralds the *Festival of Nine Lessons and Carols* from King's College Chapel.

At the east end of the main chapel building, you can see the beautiful painting *The Adoration of the Magi* by Peter Paul Reubens. It is a fitting altarpiece for the chapel.

In June 1974, a vandal with a coin scratched letters half a metre high across the centre of the painting. The scratches were deep enough to threaten the painting's integrity. It was immediately removed and art experts were called in to examine the damage. No expense was spared. Eventually, the experts reported that although the damage was severe, they were certain that it could be fully repaired.

The local Cambridge newspaper announced, 'Damaged masterpiece to be fully restored.'

This could be the headline of God's purpose for mankind. His image has been damaged by the graffiti of sin. At great personal cost, God has made restoration possible. He has begun the process now. One day he will complete it.

See what great love the Father has lavished on us, that we should be called children of God! And that is what we are! The reason the world does not know us is that it did not know him. Dear friends, now we are children of God, and what we will be has not yet been made known. But we know that when Christ appears, we shall be like him, for we shall see him as he is. All who have this hope in him purify themselves, just as he is pure.

(1 John 3:1–3)

One day we will be everything that God intended us to be.

That has to be *an identity to die for.*

## Questions

1 Why do you think that questions of identity and self-image are so prominent today?
2 Read James 1:23–24. What do these verses tell us about the Bible? How should it shape the way we read the Bible?
3 Reread the section on 'humble dignity' ('God made us to have humble dignity'). What does this tell us about the image of God? How should it affect the way we treat people?
4 Look at the definitions of sin quoted from Spurgeon and Bunyan. What do they reveal? Do you agree with these definitions?
5 Read through the first three chapters of Ephesians and make a list of the blessings recorded there.

Part 1

# I AM WHAT GOD HAS MADE ME

While I was in my teens, someone gave me a copy of *Tortured for Christ* by Richard Wurmbrand, and I devoured it. Wurmbrand was imprisoned for fourteen years by the Communist authorities in Romania because he refused to stop preaching about Jesus. He was willing to sacrifice everything for the Saviour he loved – and to do so with a joyful heart and a wry smile:

> It was strictly forbidden to preach to other prisoners. It was understood that whoever was caught doing this received a severe beating. A number of us decided to pay the price for the privilege of preaching, so we accepted their terms. It was a deal; we preached and they beat us. We were happy preaching. They were happy beating us, so everyone was happy.[1]

Wurmbrand spoke about Christ as his greatest treasure. I once heard a recording of a sermon that he had preached after his release. It went something like this:

> There were nights when I would sit in my prison cell – cold, hungry and in pain. And there in the darkness I would sing songs of joy. They could take my comforts and my possessions. They could take my dignity and my health. They could take my wife and my children. They could even take my life. But they could not take my Jesus from me. They could not take the touch of his nail-pierced hand from my life.[2]

Richard Wurmbrand was invincible because he had discovered 'an identity to die for'. All the things that had been taken from him were still important to him, but they were not the core of his identity. Knowing Jesus trumped everything else, making him invincible in the midst of terrible suffering.

In chapters 2–4, we will explore how Jesus changes everything.

We will be amazed by God's grace. We will also, though, plumb the depths before we ascend the heights of this grace, the grace that turns rebels into sons and daughters (see chapter 2).

We will begin to survey some of the treasures that our Father has planned to lavish on his children. We will discover salvation's song and learn that God does not want us to be suffocated by guilt or shame (see chapter 3).

Finally, we will explore what it means for us to exhibit the family likeness. Our new identity needs to show through (see chapter 4).

# 2

# Undeservedly rescued

## Ephesians 2:1–10

### A zoo of lusts

Tucked away at the back of the Eagle and Child pub in the city of Oxford is a room where Mr Middle Earth witnessed Mr Narnia.

It was in this room that a noteworthy literary group held their meetings. J. R. R. Tolkien, creator of *The Lord of the Rings*, set in the imaginary lands of Middle Earth, was a Christian believer whose faith shaped his world view. C. S. Lewis, for whom the Chronicles of Narnia stories still lay in the future, was a sceptic. Tolkien and Lewis both taught in the English faculty at Oxford University and it was here that they founded the informal literary society known as The Inklings.

Lewis had been baptized in the Church of Ireland but fell away from faith in his adolescence. He became an atheist at the age of fifteen, although he later admitted that he was angry with God for not existing.[1]

Through the works of George MacDonald, Lewis returned to theism, but it was the influence of Tolkien that led him back to Christianity. After resisting the Christian faith, he reluctantly bowed the knee to Christ.

You must picture me alone in that room at Magdalen, night after night, feeling, whenever my mind lifted even for a second from my work, the steady, unrelenting approach of Him whom I so earnestly desired not to meet. That which I greatly feared had at last come upon me. In the Trinity Term of 1929 I gave in, and admitted that God was God, and knelt and prayed: perhaps, that night, the most dejected and reluctant convert in all England.[2]

Part of his conversion experience was the recognition of the sin from which he was unable to extricate himself.

> For the first time I examined myself with a seriously practical purpose. And there I found what appalled me; a zoo of lusts, a bedlam of ambitions, a nursery of fears, a harem of fondled hatreds. My name was legion.[3]

Like Legion, the demon-possessed man in the Bible, he recognized that he was helpless to change his own heart (Mark 5:1–20). As in the story, however, Jesus delivered him from the grip of inner evil.

Like the demoniac, Lewis had come to experience grace.

## Digging down low to build high

My identity as a Christian is shaped by my experience of grace.

'Grace' is probably the most important word in the Christian vocabulary. It is grace that best describes the heart of God towards lost and helpless people. Grace rescues and releases. Grace connects us with God in an eternal and unbreakable relationship of love. Grace perseveres and protects us until the morning comes and the dark shadows flee away.

Before we can understand grace, we must grasp the atrocity of sin.

This is, of course, very countercultural. The received wisdom of our age is that we need to minimize our imperfections and maximize our worthiness. 'Sin' is often seen as an unhelpful and offensive word. The Christian message, it is argued, must be stripped of anything that might undermine our self-esteem. The author Robert Schuller writes,

> In a theology that starts with an uncompromising respect for each person's pride and dignity, I have no right to ever preach a sermon or write an article that would offend the self-respect and violate the self-dignity of a listener or reader. Any minister, religious leader, writer or reporter who stoops to a style, a

strategy, a substance, or a spirit that fails to show respect for his or her audience is committing an insulting sin. Every human being must be treated with respect; self-esteem is his sacred right.[4]

We will surely agree that every human being should be treated with dignity and respect. However, if we ignore the 'zoo of lusts', 'bedlam of ambitions', 'nursery of fears' and 'harem of fondled hatreds' that exist in our hearts, we will never come to understand the grace of God that has overcome our rebellious reluctance and conquered our sinful self-centredness.

Bishop J. C. Ryle begins his monumental book *Holiness* with the words:

He who wishes to attain right views about Christian holiness must begin by examining the vast and solemn subject of sin. He must dig down very low, if he would build high. A mistake here is most mischievous.[5]

We cannot begin to understand our identity in Christ unless we understand grace, and we cannot understand grace unless we understand sin.

Paul would agree with this. Ephesians 2:1–10 is one of the best-known passages in the whole epistle, and here Paul gives us a classic description of how grace works.

## Amazing depths (Ephesians 2:1–3)

Paul begins with a painfully honest description of what we were before God's grace transformed us:

As for you, you were dead in your transgressions and sins, in which you used to live when you followed the ways of this world and of the ruler of the kingdom of the air, the spirit who is now at work in those who are disobedient. All of us also lived among them at one time, gratifying the cravings of our

flesh and following its desires and thoughts. Like the rest, we were by nature deserving of wrath.
(Ephesians 2:1–3)

This is not a description of a singularly obnoxious group of people such as war criminals or child molesters; it applies to the whole of humanity, whether atheists or archbishops, philanderers or philanthropists, terrorists or teachers. It is relevant to every one of us.

Before God's grace invaded our lives, we were marked out in three ways.

## 1 We were dead in our transgressions and sins

Back in Genesis, Adam experienced an intimate and unclouded relationship with God. Fellowship with God was the essence of life. When Adam sinned, he died spiritually. He still walked, talked and had a pulse, but he was cut off from the life of God. This was true of all of us. Spiritual death means that we, too, were alienated from God.

Think of a cut flower. It may still look alive, but, separated from the stem, it is only a matter of time before it withers and dies. This was our condition. We may have been respectable and religious, but we too were spiritually dead. Something was missing. We could not change our condition, just as dead people cannot bring about their own resurrection.

This lifeless state was brought about by 'transgression' and 'sin', transgression being an act of deliberate disobedience, and sin a failure to live up to a required standard. Our hostility towards God separated us from spiritual health and well-being, which could only be found in fellowship with him.

> But your iniquities have separated
>   you from your God;
> your sins have hidden his face from you,
>   so that he will not hear.
> (Isaiah 59:2)

That in itself is pretty shocking, but there is more.

## 2 We were enslaved in a prison cell with a triple lock

We were helpless – held captive by forces that we were powerless to defeat.

We were enslaved by 'the world', which here refers to humanity in rebellion against God. The world attempts to push God to the margins and refute any claims he might make on our lives. We were part of this rebellion, blinded and oblivious to God.

More than that, we were also enslaved by the devil: the 'ruler of the kingdom of the air'. Our jailer is a vile, vicious, aggressive enemy who will do all in his power to keep us caged up. He blinds us to our true need and keeps us content in our spiritually dead condition.

Finally, we were enslaved by our own sinful natures. We were deliberately disobedient, passionately 'gratifying the cravings of our flesh and following its desires and thoughts'. The problem was not just 'out there', as if we were somehow merely reluctant victims. We were wholehearted and enthusiastic renegades. We were born as rebels with clenched fists.

This triple lock makes it impossible for us to break free. Think of the most wretched slavery you can imagine, whether it is slavery to vice, drugs or pornography. Spiritually, we were just as helpless and impotent to free ourselves.

Which brings us to the final description of our condition.

## 3 We were under God's condemnation

Before grace came, we were, 'by nature deserving of wrath' (Ephesians 2:3). As rebels against our Creator, we faced his just and terrible wrath, or anger.

The concept of God's wrath upsets modern sentiments. Haven't we long outgrown such primitive ideas? Doesn't this make God harsh and vindictive, frustrated and fuming? But the wrath of God toward sin and sinners is clearly and widely taught in the Bible. Our aversion to the idea stems from the fact that we confuse God's wrath with human anger. Wrath is not a fit of pique or an outbreak of vindictive anger. It is God's personal, righteous, consistent and settled hatred of everything that is hostile to his nature, or that spoils his creation.

Jim Packer summarizes it like this: 'God's wrath in the Bible is never the capricious, self-indulgent, irritable, morally ignoble thing that human anger so often is. It is, instead, a right and necessary reaction to objective moral evil.'[6]

John Stott describes it as: 'his steady, unrelenting, unremitting, uncompromising antagonism to evil in all its forms and manifestations'.[7]

God must act justly and judge sin. Otherwise, God would not be God.

## Why can't we see?

As a theology student, I had to write two essays a week. It was normal practice for the students in the supervision class to each read their essay to the tutor and the other students. On one occasion I had to read an essay on Paul's understanding of grace. I covered all the necessary bases, but it ended up sounding like a bit of a sermon!

My supervisor was a brilliant academic. He had studied at several prestigious universities, earned a galaxy of degrees and published several very worthy tomes.

When I finished reading the essay, he looked puzzled.

'Of course, I understand what you have written,' he said. 'I understand that Paul believed those things about sin and the cross – I understand them, but I don't get them. They just don't seem to make sense.'

I was shocked at his lack of comprehension of truths that I had grasped and delighted in since I had become a Christian aged eleven. How could this brilliant academic fail to see what seemed so patently obvious?

In my personal devotions the next morning, I was reading Ephesians 2 and the penny dropped. He could not see because he was spiritually dead – he taught theology but described himself as a 'soft agnostic'. The truth makes no sense until we have eyes to see.

Once we were all in this place.

## Amazing heights (Ephesians 2:4–7)

Having plumbed the depths, Paul lifts us to the heights, thankfully. God broke into our lives and transformed our situation. Now I have an entirely new identity.

> But because of his great love for us, God, who is rich in mercy, made us alive with Christ even when we were dead in transgressions – it is by grace you have been saved. And God raised us up with Christ and seated us with him in the heavenly realms in Christ Jesus, in order that in the coming ages he might show the incomparable riches of his grace, expressed in his kindness to us in Christ Jesus.
> (Ephesians 2:4–7)

In place of death, God has given me life. Instead of captivity, he has granted me freedom. He has replaced condemnation with reconciliation. Notice that God is the subject of all the verbs. He did all this, and I was merely the undeserving recipient of his actions.

### He made us alive

He gave us the gift of spiritual life. We did not 'turn over a new leaf' or 'try harder' to be good. A Christian is not a person who has gone through a twelve-step programme of self-reformation, but a new creation in Christ, re-created in his image.

I think of Dave.

If we had lived on Merseyside, Dave would have been called a 'scally'. The dictionary defines this as 'a roguish, self-assured young person'. That was Dave all right!

He had no connections with Christians, but something drew him to our church. After several months, he asked to see me. He was trembling as he came into my study. Before we could exchange any polite banalities, he came straight to the point.

> 'I am such a sinner. I can't stop swearing. Every time I come to church, I promise myself that I will never come again, because I feel so bad about myself. But that doesn't work. So, I've made

25

a pact with God. I'm going to try and clean up my mouth and then maybe God will accept me and I'll feel better. What do you think?'

'Listen, mate,' I responded, 'you have it the wrong way around. You can't do a patch-up job and earn God's forgiveness and acceptance. That's why Jesus came. That's why Jesus died. You come as you are. God promises to accept you just as you are. He will change you and will clean up your mouth.'

We talked late into the night and, before Dave left, God had given him new life. One of the first signs was a sanitized vocabulary! Dave wept, and so did half of the congregation, when at his baptism he described the way that God had made him alive in Christ.

God's grace can transform academics like C. S. Lewis, and scallies like Dave.

## He raised us up and seated us in the heavenly realms

After the humiliation of his Son on the cross, God the Father exalted him to his right hand. This is the place of highest accomplishment, honour and worth. Because we are 'in Christ', we too have been exalted with him and are seated with him in the heavenly realms.

To be 'in Christ' is to participate in all that Christ has done. We share his position and his accomplishments. All that belongs to him has come to belong to us. Our feet are still on the earth, but spiritually we are seated with him. His treasures are our treasures. His destiny is our destiny. Grace has totally transformed our status and identity.

Think of the analogy of marriage. When Edrie and I were married, she became mine and I became hers. My small library of theological books became hers. Her vast collection of cordon bleu cookery books became mine. Or think of the French girl who, on marrying an Englishman, changed her nationality. When asked what difference it made, she replied, 'From now on I am on the victorious side at the Battle of Waterloo!' We are identified with Jesus in his victory too.

This is our future destiny.

Adam was created to reign as God's steward on earth. But sin forfeited this. Jesus, the last Adam, won it back. He will reign for ever, and we will reign with him. This is our ultimate vocation and our final destination.

> They will see his face, and his name will be on their foreheads.
> There will be no more night. They will not need the light of a
> lamp or the light of the sun, for the Lord God will give them
> light. And they will reign for ever and ever.
> (Revelation 22:4–5)

We often forget our identity in Christ. Sin, suffering or the distractions of life warp our thinking and cause us to forget. We need, deliberately and intentionally, to fill our minds with the truth.

Listen to John Stott:

> We must keep reminding ourselves what we have and are in
> Christ. One of the great purposes of daily Bible reading,
> meditation and prayer is . . . to remember who and what we
> are. We need to say to ourselves: 'Once I was a slave, but God
> has made me a son and put the Spirit of His Son into my heart.
> How can I turn back to the old slavery?'[8]

## Amazing grace (Ephesians 2:8–10)

Why did God do this? Paul's answer is clear:

> For it is by grace you have been saved, through faith – and this
> is not from yourselves, it is the gift of God – not by works, so
> that no one can boast. For we are God's handiwork, created in
> Christ Jesus to do good works, which God prepared in advance
> for us to do.
> (Ephesians 8–10)

Here is the heart of the gospel.

Grace alone. Grace is love that sees and cares, that stoops and rescues. It is more than a sentiment or a good intention. It is a deliberate decision to act, no matter what the cost might be.

27

In the Bible, grace is directed towards the people described in the first three verses of Ephesians 2. It is freely given to rebels. The only thing we bring to the table is the sin we have to be saved from.

But Jesus had to pay a colossal price to change our condition, transform our status and alter our identity. Grace is free, but it is certainly not cheap. He took responsibility for our sinful rebellion against God and bore the consequences that we had earned, willingly placing himself under the fierce white-hot heat of God's wrath. For three hours on the cross, his soul hurtled away into the outer darkness of God's holy hatred of evil. Out of that darkness he cried, 'My God, my God, why have you forsaken me?' (Mark 15:34).

Robert Murray M'Cheyne explains that cry:

He was without any comforts of God – no feeling that God loved him – no feeling that God pitied him – no feeling that God supported him.

God was his sun before – now that sun became all darkness.

All that God had been to him before was taken from him now.

Ah! This is the hell which Christ suffered. I feel like a little child casting a stone into a deep ravine and waiting to hear it fall and never hearing it hit the bottom – it is too deep.

The ocean of Christ's sufferings is unfathomable.

He was forsaken in the place of sinners. If you close with him as your Saviour, you will never be forsaken . . . 'My God, my God, why hast thou forsaken me?'

And the answer? For me – for me.[9]

One hot and glorious summer afternoon, my two sons, both under five, disappeared to the bottom of the garden. When they reappeared, they had stripped down to their underpants and bedecked themselves with the verdant leaves they had found in the rhubarb patch.

'Look at us – we are the rhubarb boys,' they shouted.

My wife took a photo and today, over thirty years later, it still sits in pride of place on the dressing table. When I look at it, I am overwhelmed with a sense of love for those two little boys, now grown men. I honestly think that I would be willing to give my own life to protect them from suffering.

On the cross, God stood by while his only beloved Son was mocked and crucified. More than that, he participated in Calvary as he laid our sins on Christ's sinless shoulders and then poured out his fierce wrath on the head of his own Son. He condemned his Son for our lusting, hating, lying, despising and neglecting.

He did it for rebels like you and me.

That is grace.

## Many stories become one story

Last weekend we celebrated seven baptisms in our church. We heard seven moving descriptions of God's grace. Some individuals had been brought up in Christian homes and could not remember when they had first heard the good news about Jesus. Others had only recently heard that Jesus came to save sinners. One guy had even met Jesus during a service in a cow shed!

Every story was different. And yet every story was the same. I was lost and Jesus found me. I was blind and now I can see. I was in prison and Jesus set me free.

Where does my self-understanding and identity begin as a Christian? It is both simple and profound: I was a helpless sinner who deserved nothing from God but condemnation and hell. By God's grace alone, I have been ransomed, healed, restored and forgiven, and I am now the recipient of every conceivable spiritual blessing. God's grace has given repentant sinners every spiritual blessing in Christ.

As the candidates came out of the water, we sang John Newton's great hymn, 'Amazing Grace'.

Newton was such a wicked man that even his fellow slave traders would have nothing to do with him. Then God's grace invaded his life. It began by showing him his sin and helplessness, before it led him to Christ and the joy of salvation. He wrote,

'Twas grace that taught my heart to fear
And grace my fears relieved
How precious did that grace appear
The hour I first believed.[10]

As an old man, he had the words of Deuteronomy placed on his mantlepiece: 'And thou shalt remember that thou wast a bondman [slave] in the land of Egypt, and the LORD thy God redeemed thee' (15:15 KJV).

He knew that his identity depended on understanding what he once was, and what grace had now made him.

Newton never forgot it, and neither should we.

## Questions

1 The quote from C. S. Lewis refers to 'a zoo of lusts, a bedlam of ambitions, a nursery of fears, a harem of fondled hatreds'. Compare this list with Paul's description of the acts of the flesh in Galatians 5:19–21. What does this teach us about the nature of sin?

2 Why do we struggle with the concept of the wrath of God?

3 What does it mean to be 'in Christ'? Make a list of references to this in Ephesians. What do the verses of Romans 8:1; 1 Corinthians 1:30; Galatians 2:20; and Colossians 2:9–10 teach us about this?

4 How should our ultimate destiny affect our current view of ourselves?

5 How should the idea of grace shape our self-understanding and identity?

# 3

# Unbelievably blessed

## Ephesians 1:3–14

### Meet Sally

Sally's husband, Jim, was a hard-working farmer. He and Sally were blessed with a large family and their door was open to all. Like Tolkien's valley retreat in Rivendell, the home was a cure for weariness, fear and sadness, and it orbited around Sally, a natural homemaker.

But Sally had a secret.

Years before, she had lost a child. She was six months' pregnant and the doctor had warned her about overdoing things. She had tried to follow his orders, of course, but it is difficult when you are surrounded by demanding toddlers. One day the worst happened. She was admitted to hospital, but nothing could be done to rescue the little life.

Sally was completely innocent of any wrongdoing, but that was certainly not how she felt. She experienced paralyzing feelings of guilt that disturbed her sleep and devastated her appetite. Her emotions fluctuated between fear and numbness. It was like being in a fog. The pain was ever present and seemingly endless. It's bad enough to lose a baby, but when you blame yourself, the weight of guilt seems unbearable.

Of course, the real problem was grief, but under its lash, she had convinced herself that she was to blame. This was her secret. Behind a smiling face lay a heart overwhelmed with guilt.

When I got to know Sally, she was in her fifties. She had learned to cope with the burden, but there were still times when it returned with a vengeance. Sally had been a Christian for many years, having trusted Jesus to forgive her sins. Yet the sense of guilt weighed heavily on her. It warped her identity and destroyed the joy she should have experienced as a child of God.

Sally's case was extreme. She eventually reached a place where she recognized that the guilt she felt was irrational. She came to enjoy the sweet fruits of forgiveness but it was not easy.

Sensitive consciences may suffer from phantom guilt. We are familiar with the phenomenon of phantom pain, the sort that amputees sometimes feel. The nerve endings of the amputated area send signals to the brain as if the limb were still there. Phantom pain is feeling pain where it shouldn't be felt. This is what happens in the experience of phantom guilt. It is the guilt we feel for a sin we did not commit.

## Guilt and shame

Phantom guilt is irrational, but real guilt and the shame that follows close on its heels are not. I have permission to tell Sally's story, but there are numerous other examples that I might cite. I have met Christians who have been paralyzed by guilt and continue to dwell on what God has chosen to forget. Others are weighed down by shame. They know they have been forgiven but are convinced that there is no way back into the intimacy they once enjoyed with God.

There is nothing more toxic for our sense of identity than guilt and shame. These feelings become the lens through which we view ourselves. They shape our emotions and make us feel insecure, worthless and inadequate.

Guilt is feeling bad about what we do. It is an awareness of failure against a standard and, usually, tied to a particular action. I feel bad because I did something bad. For the moment, my relationship with God is spoilt.

Listen to David:

When I kept silent,
my bones wasted away
through my groaning all day long.

32

For day and night
　your hand was heavy on me;
my strength was sapped
　as in the heat of summer.
(Psalm 32:3–4)

Even when we confess our sin and believe that we are forgiven, we are still susceptible to shame. Shame is feeling bad about who we are. It is a sense of failure before the eyes of someone else. Shame eats away at our self-identity, like acid. We scold ourselves, saying, 'You did something bad because you are bad. You may be forgiven, but you still did it! What does that show about you? How many times did you fail in the same area in the past? God may not give up on you, but you will always be a second-class member of his family.'

The answer to both guilt and shame is deliberately to turn our attention away from ourselves and focus on God and his purposes for us. It is only by doing this that we can arm ourselves against this vicious duo.

In Ephesians 1:3–14 Paul takes us to the heart of the triune God and celebrates his grace. We discover a God who has loved us with an everlasting love. Would such a God want his children to be stranded in the grip of guilt or suffocated by shame?

This passage is a rhapsody of praise and a song of salvation, revealing our true identity as Christians. On our darkest days, when guilt and shame almost overwhelm us, we need to sing salvation's song.

## Chosen by a loving Father

The source of all our blessings is the God and Father of our Lord Jesus Christ.

Praise be to the God and Father of our Lord Jesus Christ, who has blessed us in the heavenly realms with every spiritual blessing in Christ. For he chose us in him before the creation of the world to be holy and blameless in his sight. In love he predestined us for adoption to sonship through Jesus Christ, in accordance with his pleasure and will – to the praise of his glorious grace, which he has freely given us in the One he loves. (Ephesians 1:3–6)

God delights in granting us 'every spiritual blessing'. He holds nothing back, but freely grants to us everything necessary for our spiritual good. He does not ignore our physical needs – we are encouraged to pray for daily bread – but the emphasis is on spiritual prosperity rather than material gain.

How did this come about?

Salvation began in eternity and in the mind of the Father. We must avoid any idea that through his death, a merciful Son had to persuade a reluctant Father to love us. The Father does not love us because Christ died for us; Christ died for us because the Father loved us (John 3:16; 1 John 4:10). God delights in saving rebels. One translation puts it like this: 'God decided in advance to adopt us into his own family by bringing us to himself through Jesus Christ. This is what he wanted to do, and it gave him great pleasure' (Ephesians 1:5 NLT).

When you think about it, this is mind-blowing. What was God doing in eternity? We know that the Father loved the Son with an eternal love – he was the darling of the Father's heart. But more than that, God loved us and made plans to rescue us from our sin. Before God spoke to bring the cosmos into existence, he loved us. He knew that we would rebel and that he would have to pay an outrageous price for our rescue, yet he still loved us.

What does this truth do for our self-understanding? If God loved us with that kind of love, it is clear that he does not want us to wallow in guilt and shame. We are completely secure in the knowledge of his love.

God's purpose in choosing us was to make us holy in his sight (Ephesians 1:4). When I feel condemned and worthless, I need to remember that in God's sight, I am blameless. He sees me in Christ and clothed in all his merits.

Just south of Birmingham lie the much-loved Lickey Hills where I proposed to my wife. If you look in one direction, you can see the rolling Worcestershire countryside. If you turn 180 degrees, you see the city of Birmingham, like the new Jerusalem coming down from heaven (or so I like to think!). You cannot see them both at the same time, however. If you look at the city, you cannot see the countryside. If you look at the countryside, you cannot see the city.

When we trust Christ, God puts our sins behind his back. He looked our sin full in the face and poured out his condemnation for it on Calvary. When he looks at us now, there is no condemnation.

It doesn't end there. When he looks at us, he sees us in Christ. All the merits of Jesus have been placed in our account. We are clothed in the righteousness of Christ. It is not that we have been given a second chance to try harder. We have been given the full package – the total righteousness of Christ.

God, whose plans are invincible, chose to do this before the creation of the world. It is therefore completely certain.

## There is still more

He chose us for adoption (Ephesians 1:5).

This is the highest privilege of all. The Son dwells in the infinite embrace of the Father's love, and we are drawn into that embrace.

Like the prodigal son, we stumble home, hoping for a humble refuge in the servant's quarters. Instead, we find ourselves seated at the highest table. The Father does not receive us on sufferance – he yearns for us to return and rejoices when we do so. We are not on probation. The prodigal son still smelled of the pigsty, but the father did not mention the smell. He put clean robes on top of rags, a ring on a dirty finger and clean sandals on smelly feet.

Adoption is the doorway into magnificent blessing:

Because you are his sons, God sent the Spirit of his Son into our hearts, the Spirit who calls out, 'Abba, Father.' So you are

no longer a slave, but God's child; and since you are his child,
God has made you also an heir.
(Galatians 4:6–7)

I have access to God and can call him Father. I know that all my
past debts have been paid off and that I am an heir with a secure
and glorious future. God has made a wretch his treasure.

But what if I sin?

Listen to John Stott:

> 'But what happens when and if I sin,' you may ask. 'Do I forfeit
> my sonship and cease to be God's child?' No. Think of … a
> human family. Imagine a boy being offensively rude to his
> parents … Father and son are not on speaking terms … Has
> the boy ceased to be his son? No. Their relationship is just the
> same; it is their fellowship which is broken. Relationship de-
> pends on birth; fellowship depends on behaviour. As soon as the
> boy apologizes, he is forgiven. And forgiveness restores fellow-
> ship. Meanwhile, his relationship has remained the same …
>
> And this applies to us.[1]

Nothing can ever separate me from the eternal loving embrace of
my heavenly Father.

This is the gospel, and it is enough.

It helped me survive the early days of my ministry. When I began,
around forty years ago, I had a sense of unworthiness because of
the gap between the ideals to which I aspired and the daily reality
of the battle against sin. Before preaching, a little voice would often
whisper in my ear, 'What a hypocrite you are. If only they knew what
you were really like, they would never want you to preach to them
again.'

When it became almost too much to bear, I went to see an older
pastor. I shared my sense of unworthiness with him and he listened
patiently.

When I had finished, he simply smiled and asked me, 'Have you
never heard of the gospel?'

It's a rather embarrassing question to be asked as a preacher!

'Of course, I have,' I feebly responded.

'So why don't you believe it?'

You can know the gospel, study the gospel, love the gospel and even preach the gospel, but fail to feel its force at work in your life. There is no special doctrine for leaders or no secret truth only discovered when you have been on the road for a few years. There is only the gospel. But the gospel is enough.

## Rescued by a mighty Saviour

Paul goes on to describe the way in which the Son has won all these privileges for us:

> In him we have redemption through his blood, the forgiveness of sins, in accordance with the riches of God's grace that he lavished on us. With all wisdom and understanding, he made known to us the mystery of his will according to his good pleasure, which he purposed in Christ, to be put into effect when the times reach their fulfilment – to bring unity to all things in heaven and on earth under Christ.
>
> In him we were also chosen, having been predestined according to the plan of him who works out everything in conformity with the purpose of his will, in order that we, who were the first to put our hope in Christ, might be for the praise of his glory.
> (Ephesians 1:7–12)

The Son brought about the Father's purposes and fulfilled his plans by dying to redeem his people, setting us free and rescuing us by the payment of a price.

We were slaves of sin, haunted by its presence, gripped by its power and threatened by its penalty. But Christ redeemed us from sin's bondage, so that our slate was wiped clean and we were fully and finally forgiven.

As we saw earlier, however, this was at an incredible cost, for we were redeemed by his blood.

In the Bible, blood is the symbol of violent death. Jesus' death was an abomination of mockery and blood, of pain and torture. This blood represented his life pouring on to the ground. What made it effective was that it was the blood of the one who was God incarnate. His blood achieved what God required. This is why it was the most precious thing in the universe:

> For you know that it was not with perishable things such as silver or gold that you were redeemed from the empty way of life handed down to you from your ancestors, but with the precious blood of Christ, a lamb without blemish or defect.
> (1 Peter 1:18–19)

By this act of redemption, Christ paid the price to free us from both guilt and shame.

## The power of the blood

What do we do about guilt and shame? Guilt can be a heavy burden, dragging us down.

Do you remember Dave from chapter 2? Shortly after his conversion, we discovered that he had an unrealized artistic gift. He began to draw pictures for a series of talks for children that I wanted to run based on John Bunyan's *The Pilgrim's Progress*. Dave had never heard of it, but I went through the story with him and he produced some stunning illustrations.

Christian was weighed down by the burden of his sin. Dave produced a picture of the largest rucksack I had ever seen. At first glance, that was all I could see, but on closer examination, I noticed a tiny little stick man almost hidden by the burden. When I questioned Dave, he told me, 'That was me! That's what my burden felt like!'

What is God's answer to the burden of guilt? It is the cross on which Jesus shed his blood to remove that burden.

We reached the part where John Bunyan describes Christian's arrival at the cross:

So I saw in my dream, that just as Christian came up with the cross, his burden loosed from off his shoulders, and fell from off his back; and began to tumble, and so continued to do so until it came to the mouth of the sepulchre, where it fell in, and I saw it no more.

Shortly thereafter, Christian sang his song of deliverance . . . Blessed cross! Blessed sepulchre! Blessed rather be the Man that there was put to shame for me.[2]

You can imagine how Dave enjoyed drawing that picture.

When God's Spirit convicts us of our sin, we are to come back to the cross with humble and contrite hearts. We remember the blood of Jesus and freely confess our sins without trying to justify our actions. We then need to apply the balm of Scripture to our bruised consciences. A feeling of guilt might linger for a while, but we can remind ourselves that Christ paid the price for our sin. We can meet guilt feelings with the objective promises of Scripture: 'If we confess our sins, he is faithful and just and will forgive us our sins and purify us from all unrighteousness' (1 John 1:9).

Satan loves to condemn us, but we respond with the truth – the sword of the Spirit, the Word of God.

## The smear of shame

The devil is persistent. At this point, he may well try to focus on our feelings of shame.

This can be an excruciating experience, as Lewis B. Smedes describes:

Shame is a very heavy feeling. It's a feeling that we do not measure up and maybe never will measure up to the sorts of people we are meant to be. The feeling, when we are conscious of it, gives us a vague disgust with ourselves which in turn feels like a hunk of lead in our hearts. Unhealthy shame spills into everything we are – it flops, sloshes and smears our whole being.[3]

We meet the sense of shame with the truth of Scripture, which affirms that we are beloved children in God's family, clothed in the righteousness of his Son and destined for glory. We do not have to live constantly looking over our shoulder and dwelling on past failure. Instead, we are to run the race with perseverance.

> Brothers and sisters, I do not consider myself yet to have taken hold of it. But one thing I do: forgetting what is behind and straining toward what is ahead, I press on toward the goal to win the prize for which God has called me heavenward in Christ Jesus.
> (Philippians 3:13–14)

Dale Ralph Davis expresses it like this:

> You don't go back and wallow in your guilt, relive the tragic mistake, the 'big one' which soured your life. You don't make yourself miserable by bathing your mind in the memory of your rebellion. Punching the play button and going over the whole messy episode in lurid detail as though such misery makes atonement. No, you go forward in basic simple fidelity to Yahweh from that point on.[4]

Our thinking can be confused here. Surely, we think, it would be better to fester in my sin for a while. Isn't this a necessary mark of real repentance? Don't I deserve to feel bad, as a kind of penance for my failure?

We should certainly ask God to help us to hate our sin more, but we do not need to offer our misery and shame as an atonement to supplement what Jesus did for us. Jesus redeemed us from both guilt and shame. His sacrifice on the cross covers both. His grace is sufficient for everything. It is not a drop, but a shower; not a trickle, but a flood; not a puddle, but an ocean. God is saying, 'Come back to God, and come back quickly.'

This passage from Ephesians gives us further incentive for doing this. God's ultimate plan is bigger than me. It encompasses the whole universe. One day, God will restore unity, harmony and peace to a broken and divided world (Ephesians 1:9–10). He will bring everything together under the headship of Christ. The universe will be under new management and everything will be healed (Revelation 21:1–4).

As I struggle with my sin now, I know that Jesus will make everything new. I am destined to share his throne and to reign with him. On that day I will never fall into sin again. Not only will I never sin, I will not even want to sin. No more guilt and no more shame for ever and ever!

## Sealed by the eternal Spirit

Everything that the Father planned for us, and that the Son has purchased for us, has been applied to us by the Holy Spirit. His work is as essential as that of the Father and Son, the other members of the Trinity.

And you also were included in Christ when you heard the message of truth, the gospel of your salvation. When you believed, you were marked in him with a seal, the promised Holy Spirit, who is a deposit guaranteeing our inheritance until the redemption of those who are God's possession – to the praise of his glory.
(Ephesians 1:13–14)

Paul is using two metaphors.

First, the Holy Spirit is a 'seal' (1:13). Paul preached in Ephesus, and those who believed his message were sealed with the Holy Spirit. A seal was used to brand livestock, possessions or slaves. It is like the hallmark on a piece of jewellery. God has given the Spirit as a seal. When we believe, he comes to live in us as a confirmation of our identity and an assurance of our destiny. His presence is a reminder that we belong to God and are secure in his possession.

Second, the Spirit has been given as a *pledge* (1:14). Translated from its original New Testament Greek form, this was the word Paul used to refer to the part payment of a purchase price in advance. The Spirit is a first instalment, deposit or down payment: 'Now it is God who makes both us and you stand firm in Christ. He anointed us, set his seal of ownership on us, and put his Spirit in our hearts as a deposit, guaranteeing what is to come' (2 Corinthians 1:21–22).

When we begin to experience the Spirit's work in our lives, we are beginning to get a foretaste of heaven itself. The Spirit makes us homesick for heaven as we long to enter into this inheritance. All the blessings we experience now are a mere foretaste of the glory to come. The best is yet to be.

When we sin, the Holy Spirit convicts us and makes our hearts tender and repentant. But he does not leave us stranded in condemnation. His purpose is always to bring us back to Christ, where we can find the forgiveness we need. He then assures us of our full acceptance. He bears witness with our spirits that we are children of God. He takes the promises of Scripture and seals them to our hearts.

The Spirit you received does not make you slaves, so that you live in fear again; rather, the Spirit you received brought about your adoption to sonship. And by him we cry, 'Abba, Father.' The Spirit himself testifies with our spirit that we are God's children. Now if we are children, then we are heirs – heirs of God and co-heirs with Christ, if indeed we share in his sufferings in order that we may also share in his glory. (Romans 8:15–17)

Over the years, I have met many people like Sally, struggling with the inner turmoil of guilt and failure. In some cases, like hers, it is phantom guilt. In many others, it is the real thing. Sometimes it is a very specific action that has marked a person's conscience like an ugly tattoo. It may be a denial of Christ, or an extramarital affair, or the quiet termination of an unwanted pregnancy. In other cases, it is the daily failure to overcome temptation and the despair that this brings.

Yes, we have to learn to hate sin and pray for real contrition and true repentance. But the passage we have been studying takes us into the heart of the triune God, who does not want us to be stranded in the misery of condemnation.

The Father loved us, chose us and adopted us into his family.

The Son willingly shed his blood to redeem us.

The Holy Spirit lives in us as the guarantee that one day our war with sin will be over.

As I gaze into the mirror of Scripture, the triune God tells me who he is and what he has done to rescue me. I need these truths when I feel worthless and condemned. I need them when they don't feel true. I need them when Satan tempts me to despair.

God does not want us to shoulder the burden that Christ came to bear for us. We need to hear again the words that conclude the Anglican Communion Service: 'Go in peace to love and serve the Lord.'

Living as a Christian involves the daily celebration of who I am in Christ and the deliberate decision to be what I am, the subject of our next chapter.

## Questions

1 How can we recognize the difference between real guilt and phantom guilt?
2 'God loved us and chose us in Christ before the creation of the world!' What does that truth do for our self-understanding?
3 Why are guilt and shame 'a vicious duo'? How do they differ? How do we deal with them?
4 Read Philippians 3:12–14. What do these verses tell us to do? How do we do it?
5 How does the Spirit help me when I fall into sin?

# 4

# Unimaginably transformed

## Ephesians 4:25–32

### Guess the pupil

I began my professional life as a teacher of religious education in Wiltshire. Being an RE teacher meant that most of the pupils entered my classroom for one forty-minute lesson each week. In an average week, I saw over four hundred children. That was no problem – until Parents' Evening. Suddenly I found myself confronted with the parents of pupils I could not possibly identify. To me, they were merely names on a register and marks in a book. I hope that I'm not giving away the secrets of the teaching profession, and maybe it's just RE teachers who have this problem, but each new parent presented me with a challenge: 'Who on earth is your child?'

Of course, some of the 'livelier' children were easy to remember. I had crossed swords with them and they were indelibly imprinted on my mind, but what about the quiet kids who came in just once a week and never made waves? I could have said, 'I'm sorry but I don't have a clue who your daughter is,' but that didn't feel quite right. So, instead, I played the game of guess the pupil.

Within thirty seconds of sitting down, I was watching for tell-tale signs to help me identify the child prodigy who belonged to the slightly nervous parent sitting in front of me. A physical resemblance, the lilt of a voice or a facial gesture might do it. Sometimes I was successful. At other times, I had spectacular failures.

However, the principle behind the game holds true. There should be some family likeness.

## Bearing the family likeness

We are God's children. This is our identity and there is nothing more important about us than this:

> For he chose us in him before the creation of the world to be holy and blameless in his sight. In love, he predestined us for adoption to sonship through Jesus Christ, in accordance with his pleasure and will.
> (Ephesians 1:4–5)

Notice that adoption and holiness are linked here. As an adopted child of God, I am to exhibit a growing likeness to my holy heavenly Father.

Holiness is not an optional extra reserved for a special class of Christian converts. It is the reason why God redeemed us in the first place. God rescued Israel from slavery so that it would become a kingdom of priests and a holy nation (Exodus 19:3–6). Israel was to be distinct from every other nation. Peter applies this to the church (1 Peter 2:5).

God the Father chose us in Christ before the foundation of the world, so that we should be holy (Ephesians 1:4). God the Son shed his blood to purify a people – to become his holy and pure bride (Ephesians 5:25–27). The agenda of the Holy Spirit is to transform us, so that we become holy (2 Corinthians 3: 17–18). The deliberate and determined design of the triune God is to bring a holy people into existence.

J. C. Ryle expressed it like this:

> We must be holy, because this is the one grand end and purpose for which Christ came into the world ... Jesus is a complete Saviour. He does not merely take away the guilt of the believer's sin, he does more – he breaks its power (1 Peter 1:2; Romans 8:29; 2 Timothy 1:9; Hebrews 12:10).[1]

But what does this look like? We don't need to guess. Jesus is the image of the invisible God and the exact representation of his being

(Colossians 1:15; Hebrews 1:3). He displays God's holiness perfectly. If I want to know what holiness looks like, then I can learn from Jesus. He is my older brother who perfectly exhibits the family likeness. When we look at Jesus, we see what a life of holiness should look like. God's ultimate purpose is to make us like Jesus: 'For those God foreknew he also predestined to be conformed to the image of his Son, that he might be the firstborn among many brothers and sisters' (Romans 8:29).

When I wake up in the morning, my first thought should be: 'Thank you, God, for saving me. Now, how can I be more like Jesus today? What are those areas of my life that still need work?'

Sanctification, the process of making us holy, is the slow but sure transformation of adopted children so that they bear the family likeness and begin to think, speak and act like Jesus. It is more than obeying a set of external rules. It is the inner transformation of the heart, so that we love what Jesus loves, hate what Jesus hates and begin to resemble him. It is us growing into our true identity.

## Looking like Jesus

What are the marks of such a life? What does our new identity look like?

Paul describes a Christlike life in Ephesians 4:25–32. Let's break it down:

> Therefore each of you must put off falsehood and speak truthfully to your neighbour, for we are all members of one body.
> (4:25)

Jesus always told the truth. Indeed, he was the truth incarnate (John 14:6). If we want to be like Jesus, our words will be truthful. This is a general principle, but Paul applies it particularly to the way in which we relate within the church family. If we tell lies, we are damaging those with whom we have an intimate relationship. Lying to our fellow believers is lying to the family. We lie in order to escape from an embarrassing situation, or to promote ourselves and our agenda. Children of God don't do that.

Our new identity is one of impeccable honesty and absolute trustworthiness.

> In your anger do not sin: do not let the sun go down while you are still angry, and do not give the devil a foothold.
> (4:26–27)

Jesus was angry when it was appropriate and when a lack of passion would have indicated a lack of moral perception. However, he was only ever angry on behalf of the vulnerable (Mark 3:5; 10:14), or because of the slight to his Father's glory (Matthew 21:12–13; John 2:13–22). Not all anger is sinful. There are times when our passion for righteousness will make us angry. But it is easy for anger to tip over into sin. 'Anger' is one letter short of 'danger'. We need to deal with it quickly, before the devil uses it as a bridgehead into our hearts.

Our new identity is one of appropriate passion and vigilant self-control.

> Anyone who has been stealing must steal no longer, but must work, doing something useful with their own hands, that they may have something to share with those in need.
> (4:28)

When the devil offered Jesus all the kingdoms of this world in exchange for the worship of his heart, Jesus resisted the temptation. He chose the way of poverty and the cross. He shunned the lure of the riches of this world. He preached from a borrowed boat, ate his last meal in a borrowed room and was buried in a borrowed grave. The love of money did not grip his heart. This world is materialistic and it is tempting to love things. Material possessions are not bad in themselves: God has given us all things to enjoy richly. But two questions must be asked: how did I acquire my possessions, and how do I plan to use them? Christians should be honest and create wealth that they can use to bless others. When we invest in the kingdom of God, we are investing in treasure that lasts.

I once saw the following motto on a church noticeboard: 'Do your givin', while you're livin', then you're knowin', where its goin'.'

Bad spelling but excellent theology!

Our new identity is one of diligent and overflowing generosity.

> Do not let any unwholesome talk come out of your mouths, but only what is helpful for building others up according to their needs, that it may benefit those who listen. And do not grieve the Holy Spirit of God, with whom you were sealed for the day of redemption. Get rid of all bitterness, rage and anger, brawling and slander, along with every form of malice. (4:29–31)

Jesus' words brought health and healing to the hearts of the people he met. They were words of life. In the same way, our words have power to build up and to encourage (Hebrews 10:24–25). We need to control our words, so that they minister health to others.

Also, we must avoid 'unwholesome' talk. The word used here was used elsewhere of rotten fruit. Think how one decaying apple can taint the whole bag. These are the kinds of words that are bitter and slanderous (4:31). Such words grieve the Spirit (4:30). 'Grieve' is a love word, reminding us that the Spirit is a person, not a force or an object. We should be sensitive to his promptings and submit to his directions contained in Scripture. His purpose is to make us like Jesus.

Our new identity is one of deliberate altruism and careful restraint.

> Be kind and compassionate to one another, forgiving each other, just as in Christ God forgave you. (4:32)

Jesus' ministry was marked by compassion. When he came upon the funeral of the only son of a widow, Luke tells us that his heart went out to her (Luke 7:13). In the trials of life, we may need to develop a thick skin, but this must never be at the expense of a tender heart.

One of the greatest tests of our compassion is our willingness to forgive. Once again Jesus is our great example here.

He taught the importance of forgiveness and he practised what he preached. When they threw him to the ground and began to drive nails the size of railroad spikes through his hands and feet, his lips moved in prayer. Perhaps the centurion in charge of the execution squad bent down close to hear the words. If he did, the words would have amazed him. Jesus prayed, 'Father forgive them, for they do not know what they are doing' (Luke 23:34). It may be difficult to forgive, but God does not leave us with the option of harbouring bitterness or unforgiveness (Matthew 6:14–15; Colossians 3:13). In place of an unforgiving attitude, we must be marked by kindness and compassion, the characteristics that marked Jesus out.

Our new identity is one of unconditional mercy and irresistible gentleness.

## Forgiving, as we have been forgiven

Let's consider the importance of forgiveness.

Probably the clearest hallmark of a child of God is in this area. In a fallen world, people will hurt us. Forgiveness is difficult because we continue to feel the pain of the hurt. It seems so unnatural and counterintuitive. However, there are over a hundred references to forgiveness in the Bible. It is not a subject we can easily ignore.

What is forgiveness?

Let's begin with what it is not. When we forgive, we do not approve of a sinful action or make excuses for it. We do not deny what was done or simply suppress the consequences, and we cannot guarantee to forget the hurt. If a drunk driver kills one of my children and is converted in prison and comes asking for my forgiveness, what do I do? As a child of God, I have to forgive him. Does that mean that I will forget what has happened to my child?

No, I will carry the pain for the rest of my life, even though I have forgiven the perpetrator.

Forgiveness means to wipe the slate clean, to pardon and to cancel the debt. When we forgive someone, we are making certain promises:

> I promise that I will not indulge myself in thinking about this incident. I will not bring it up and use it against you. I will not talk to others about it. I will not seek after revenge. I will not keep a record of wrong. I will not allow it to stand between us and hinder our personal relationship. I will only ever desire good for you.

We must forgive, because it is commanded and our own forgiveness depends on it. We disqualify ourselves from being forgiven if we are so hardened in bitterness that we cannot and will not forgive others. It is vital for maintaining our spiritual health.

There are occasions when this is a massive challenge. We have been so deeply hurt that forgiveness seems utterly impossible. In such circumstances, we need to return to the experience of grace that we thought about in chapters 2 and 3. I never get beyond this. I needed grace on the first day that I believed. I will need it on the day that I die. If I refuse to forgive, I show that I have not grasped my indebtedness. An unforgiving spirit will produce a bitter heart. I have met Christians who have been disfigured by a cherished bitterness. An embittered pastor once quoted the words of Yitzhak Zuckerman, the Jewish resistance fighter, to describe his own condition: 'If you could lick my heart it would poison you.'

Unforgivingness takes us to some dark places and it leads to a disintegration of Christian identity.

## The beauty of Jesus

Perhaps, at this point, Paul realizes that the kind of life that he has been describing is a huge challenge to any one of us. It is one thing to recognize our new identity in Christ, but quite another to begin to live it out.

Who can control temper or tongue? Who can forgive the indefensible? Who can love like Jesus loved?

In order to reinforce his words, therefore, Paul takes the people of Ephesus to the heart of holiness and reminds them that they are God's children: 'Follow God's example, therefore, as dearly loved children, and live a life of love, just as Christ loved us and gave himself up for us as a fragrant offering and sacrifice to God' (Ephesians 5:1–2).

Paul gives us two commands and two incentives.

The first command is to follow God's example. Paul uses the Greek word for 'example', from which we derive the English word *mimic*. We are to be like God. His character is to be reproduced in us. We are to be holy as he is holy. Adam was made in God's image. Sin marred that image. Grace restores it.

What will this look like?

The answer is seen in the second imperative: we are to walk in the way of love. We are to follow the example of Jesus and to live a life of love. If love is at the heart of the revelation of the glory of God (Exodus 34:6–7), then it is perfectly exemplified in the life of Jesus, who poured out his life for us. Jesus is both our Saviour and our model. Just as he humbled himself, so we too are to be marked out by a life of humility, service and sacrifice.

In his last sermon at the Keswick Convention in 2007, an aged and frail John Stott preached on Christian discipleship:

> I want to share with you where my mind has come to rest as I approach the end of my pilgrimage on earth, and it is – God wants his people to become like Christ, Christlikeness is the will of God for the people of God.[2]

In his magnificent book, *The Hole in Our Holiness,* Kevin DeYoung takes us to the heart of the matter:

> We see all the virtues of holiness perfectly aligned in Christ.
> He was always gentle, but never soft.
> He was bold, but never brash.
> He was pure, but never prudish.

He was full of mercy, but never at the expense of justice.
He was full of truth, but not at the expense of grace.
In everything he was submissive to his Father, and he gave
    everything for his sheep.
He obeyed his parents, kept the law of God, and forgave
    his enemies.
He never lusted, never coveted and never lied.
In all that Jesus Christ did, during his whole life and
    especially as his life came to an end, he loved God with
    his whole being and loved his neighbour as himself.
If somewhere down the road you forget the Ten
    Commandments or can't recall the fruit of the Spirit
    or don't remember any particular attribute of God, you
    can still remember what holiness is by simply
    remembering his name.[3]

## Our incentives

What are our incentives to live out the implications of our identity?
First, Paul reminds the Ephesians of what he has already told them. We are partakers of God's nature and members of his family. As dearly loved children, we must live in such a way that we please our Father. When people look at our lives, they should not be confused about our identity. Even suffering is part of our Father's gracious and wise discipline, to transform us into the likeness of Jesus:

Endure hardship as discipline; God is treating you as his children. For what children are not disciplined by their father? If
you are not disciplined – and everyone undergoes discipline –
then you are not legitimate, not true sons and daughters at all.
Moreover, we have all had human fathers who disciplined us
and we respected them for it. How much more should we
submit to the Father of spirits and live! They disciplined us for
a little while as they thought best; but God disciplines us
for our good, in order that we may share in his holiness. No
discipline seems pleasant at the time, but painful. Later on,

however, it produces a harvest of righteousness and peace for those who have been trained by it.
(Hebrews 12:7–11)

Let me quote from my first book:

> In the meantime, God is at work in the long, laborious process of creating character. He demands our full cooperation; we are to 'work out our salvation with fear and trembling' (Philippians 2:12). Like a soldier in a battle or an athlete in a race or a boxer in the ring, we are to work hard at Christian discipleship. We are to 'put to death' our old desires and passions, and feed our new longings and spiritual cravings.
>
> For his part, God is committed to us and determined to change us to become more like Jesus. For this, he uses a number of tools. And suffering is probably the sharpest tool in his box. Trials are necessary in the creation of character.[4]

Second, we constantly remind ourselves of the sacrifice that Jesus made on our behalf: 'he loved us and gave himself up for us as a fragrant offering and sacrifice to God' (Ephesians 5:2).

The cross is the place where free grace is demonstrated and salvation is won at enormous cost. It does not give us a second chance to try harder and do better. It satisfies God's righteous anger against our sin and saves us from punishment, death and hell. It changes our identity and our destiny, but it is also a model and a motif of the way we should now live. The cross is the fullest possible expression of selfless love. When we see such love in action, we are forced to admit that holiness is not some strange other-worldly weirdness. It does not dehumanize us. Rather it makes us more fully human. It is not sombre, but stunning. It does not repel but attracts. It is marked out by love and joy, grace and sacrifice. It is seen in a man pouring out his life, not for his friends but for his enemies.

There is nothing more compelling and life-transforming than to gaze on the beauty of Jesus: 'And we all, who with unveiled faces contemplate the Lord's glory, are being transformed into his image with ever-increasing glory, which comes from the Lord, who is the Spirit' (2 Corinthians 3:18).

Our battle with sin is not 'out there'. Rather, it is inward and intensely personal. The battleground is my heart. How do we secure the allegiance of the heart? Not by cajoling and threatening. Not by launching ourselves on some kind of unhealthy guilt trip. We win our hearts by looking again at Jesus and falling in love with him.

Yesterday morning, my fellow pastor in Bath, Clover Todman, preached a sermon from John 10. Three times, Jesus tells us how we can recognize the Good Shepherd – he is the one who lays down his life for the flock (John 10:11, 14–15, 17). To make his point, he showed us a picture of a toddler playing happily in the garden. Mum is proudly looking on. Suddenly a new image appears on the screen. It is a ferocious and bloodthirsty wolf. The child is in danger. What does the mother do?

> There is only one way this is ever going to go. There is only one outcome. She will run and place herself between the child and danger. At the cost of her own life, she will do everything she can to rescue him.
>
> The Good Shepherd did that for his sheep. Jesus did that on the cross. And he did it, not for innocent children but for rebels. And what made him do it? The same thing that motivated the mother. Love. Amazing, sacrificial and costly love.[5]

It was exactly what my heart needed.

Knowing that we are loved with such a love will transform us and give us a passion to be like Jesus. He died to give me my identity as a child of God. As I consider his sacrifice, it makes me willing to die for my own selfish desires and passions. His death has given me *an identity to die for*.

As we survey the wondrous cross, on which the young prince of glory died, I am brought to echo the words of the great hymn writer Isaac Watts:

Were the whole realm of nature mine,
That were a present far too small;
Love so amazing, so divine.[6]

In my early days as a teacher, I was not always successful at matching parent with child.

When our friends look at us, do they see the character of our Father clearly demonstrated? Do they sense the love and grace of our Elder Brother? Does the way we live match our new identity?

## Questions

1  What do you understand by the word 'holiness'?

2  What does Ephesians 4:25 - 5:2 teach us about the tongue? Compare it with James 3:3–8. In what ways do our words reveal our character?

3  Look at Kevin DeYoung's description of the character of Christ. In what ways should this be reproduced in our lives? What does it mean to look like Jesus?

4  Why do we find forgiveness so difficult? How can we learn to forgive?

5  Read Hebrews 12:7–11. How does God use suffering to mould our characters and make us like Jesus? How should we respond?

Part 2

# I AM A PART OF
# A NEW COMMUNITY

# Community and identity

I once heard a sermon entitled 'When God is not enough'. I think it was deliberately designed to be provocative – a preacher's opening gambit to secure the attention of his congregation.

Nonetheless, the preacher made a compelling case.

His starting point was Genesis 2:18. God had created a faultless world in which everything was perfect and complete. However, something was missing: 'The Lord God said, "It is not good for the man to be alone. I will make a helper suitable for him"' (Genesis 2:18).

So, the Lord creates the woman to be a partner who would complete the man and act as a 'suitable helper (2:20). In this event in Eden, we see not only the creation of the first marriage and the first family, but also the first community. It is not good for this man to be alone. It is not good for any man or woman to be alone.

People need people.

When it comes to my personal identity, it is impossible to understand myself in isolation. God is relational and he made me with an inbuilt need for relationships. I was created for community. My identity is fashioned by the relationships I form. Solitary confinement is a form of punishment designed to dehumanize. We know that we can never be truly human without significant relationships. This is why loneliness is such a curse. People of all ages suffer from it; agony aunts and uncles frequently address it; the Beatles sang about it. I was made to love and to be loved. If this longing is frustrated, then my identity will be stunted.

The Christian's experience of God is personal, but it is never private. I can only become what I am meant to be within the context of the local church.

This is the theme in this second part of the book.

We will explore together the way in which God has broken down the barriers that divide people and how, through the death of his Son, he has brought about a new community made up of a new humanity (see chapter 5).

We will also investigate the relationship between calling and identity, and focus on the way that our identity is worked out as we serve one another in the local church (see chapter 6).

Finally, we will examine the way in which the focus of our worship determines our identity. We will come to see that worship is a communal activity, which flows from the Spirit-filled life of love and mutual submission (see chapter 7).

# 5

# Every barrier down

## Ephesians 2:11–22

### We belong together

Life often involves losing things.

When I heard the dire news about my grandson Abe, my first reaction was a kind of numbing grief. Sleep was elusive and food tasted like dust and ashes. I begin to think about all that had been lost. Every child represents a world of possibilities. Many of these remain unrealized, but at least you can dream. For our beautiful grandson, life could only be exceedingly limited.

One morning, Edrie confessed to me, 'I have been wondering whether I could give my life so that Abe could be normal. I know it makes no sense, but I'd do anything for him.'

Irrational – yes – but also perfectly natural. What parent or grandparent has not thought the same in the face of overwhelming heartache?

When it hits, you turn to the people you love. Our family was wonderfully supportive and so was the church.

Our brothers and sisters shared our grief and helped us to shoulder the burden that was too heavy for us to carry on our own. One particular moment stands out. We had just returned from a painful hospital visit, and I was due to preach. I sat in my study before the service, praying that God would get me through it. As I sat there, one of the students who attends our church gently knocked on the door. Rather sheepishly he came into the room and said, 'I don't know what to say to you, but I want you to know that I pray for your grandson every day.'

And then he was gone.

Little tokens of love like that were repeated a thousand times over.

I am reminded of when my wife was desperately ill:

We received phone calls and letters and cards from virtually every brand of Christian you can imagine. We received messages of support from charismatic Baptists and Reformed Anglicans. We had phone calls from traditional Pentecostals and progressive Brethren. We were encouraged by Presbyterians and Methodists and Congregationalists. People we had never met, some on the other side of the world, had heard about this pastor and the problems that he and his pregnant wife were going through, and they were rising up in a wonderful wave of concern and comfort and compassion. I would turn up at the hospital with the cards and letters, and Edrie and I would be amazed at the kindness and generosity.[1]

Life is about losing things. But God has given us brothers and sisters to share the pain. Being part of the community of the church is essential to my self-understanding and identity as a Christian.

It is good to know that you belong.

## Belonging

We all want to belong.

We live in a world shot through with division and exclusion. Of course, we can all think of the hostilities that exist on the international scene – the Middle East, the Korean Peninsula, the border between Ukraine and Russia. But there are divisions closer to home too. As I write, the Archbishop of Canterbury has just delivered his New Year message, in which he laments the deep rifts that exist in our society and our inability to disagree in an agreeable way. It is a common theme, but divisions are sometimes even more personal and pressing, tearing apart marriages and ripping open families.

The world can be a cold and forbidding place.

We often allow ourselves to be shaped by the opinions and judgment of others. This is especially true for young people because of the huge role that social media plays in the formation of their identity. So much seems to be defined by how many 'likes' they get. A tide of insensitive, harmful or cruel comments assaults them at a tender stage, when so much of their fragile self-concept is being formed. This is when they are most prone to insecurity, comparison and trying on the ill-fitting masks we spoke of earlier. It can easily lead to a sense of exclusion and alienation.

The feelings of being an outsider, of being excluded or watching from the sidelines, are all negative emotions.

By contrast, why is the identity that Jesus died to give us an identity to die for?

Because, among other things, he takes outsiders and brings them in. In place of exclusion, we find acceptance and companionship and love.

We belong.

But how did this happen?

## Keep out!

Let's begin with a nameless first-century African politician whose story is recorded by Luke in Acts 8:26–40. He was an important official in the government in the ancient kingdom of Kush (modern-day Northern Sudan). He had grown weary of the religions on offer in his homeland. They all involved the worship of inanimate blocks of wood and stone, which seemed so distant from the needs of the human heart. They were also shot through with immorality and corruption. Yes, there were plenty of religions on offer but he felt that under the surface they were all the same.

Then he discovered Judaism. Here was a God worthy of worship and a religion with high moral standards.

With mounting excitement, he made the long journey to Jerusalem. What were his hopes? Did he expect to meet this God in the temple that was dedicated to his name?

The temple in Jerusalem was a magnificent building. The outer courtyard was referred to as the Court of the Gentiles and non-Jews were allowed to enter, but that was as far as they could go. The inner courts of the temple were reserved for Jewish people. If a Gentile approached the gate to the inner court, he would be confronted with a high wall and a warning sign in Greek and Latin. He would read these ominous words written in large red letters: 'No foreigner is to go beyond the balustrade and the plaza of the temple zone. Whoever is caught doing so will have only himself to blame for his death, which will follow.'

Nothing could symbolize more graphically the division that existed between Jews and Gentiles in the first century.

This was as far as our unnamed African seeker could go. The warning was clear. If you are not a Jew, you are excluded, disqualified from any relationship with God and from any relationship with the people of God. We know from contemporary sources that, as a Gentile, he would have been excluded from the temple and told, 'You do not belong here. Keep out!'

## Invisible walls

The wall of division in the temple is long gone but there are still invisible walls running through the human heart. You can try to legislate against racism, sexism and ageism, but only God's grace can change the human heart where these demons lurk, waiting for an opportunity to show themselves.

So, is there hope for a divided world?

Yes, and it lies in the plans and purposes of God.

In Ephesians, God reveals his ultimate purpose for a divided world: 'to bring unity to all things in heaven and on earth under Christ' (1:10).

One day, Christ will reign and all divisions will disappear. The new creation will be marked out by harmony and concord. Divisions will be gone for ever.

What will this look like?

Paul's answer is remarkable. It will look like the church!

His intent was that now, through the church, the manifold wisdom of God should be made known to the rulers and authorities in the heavenly realms, according to his eternal purpose that he accomplished in Christ Jesus our Lord. (Ephesians 3:10–12)

The unity, community and love that exist in the church are a foretaste of the harmony that will one day flood the whole universe. God draws the attention of rulers and authorities in the heavenly realms to his church and says,

Look at my church! Look at her unity! Look at the way in which every barrier has been broken down! Look at how these Christians love one another! One day the whole cosmos will display this unity under the headship of Christ.

When we look at the church, we are supposed to see a foretaste of God's plan for the whole cosmos.

Ephesians 2:11–22 describes how this unity has been brought about.

## Alienation

Jesus came to create a community where divisions have been abolished and former enemies are reconciled.

Listen to John Stott:

The church as a multi-racial, multi-cultural community is like a beautiful tapestry. Its members come from a wide range of colourful backgrounds. No other human community resembles it. Its diversity and harmony are unique. It is God's new community. It is God's new society.[2]

How has this new community been brought into existence?

Paul begins by reminding the people of their status as Gentiles before they met Jesus:

Therefore, remember that formerly you who are Gentiles by birth and called 'uncircumcised' by those who call themselves

'the circumcision' (which is done in the body by human hands) – remember that at that time you were separate from Christ, excluded from citizenship in Israel and foreigners to the covenants of the promise, without hope and without God in the world.
(Ephesians 2:11–12)

Paul paints a graphic picture of exclusion.

They were the 'uncircumcised' (2:11). For Jews, circumcision was the sign of acceptance with God and a point of access into a universal brotherhood. Gentiles were referred to as 'uncircumcised dogs' and considered as little more than fuel for the flames of hell.' The wall in the temple was the most visible symbol of the hostility that Gentiles would experience on a daily basis.

They were separated from all blessings that the Messiah would bring. They had no part with the chosen people and were ignorant of all the promises that God had made to them. Worst of all, they were without hope and without God. Their religion gave no hope beyond the grave and they had no relationship with the true and living God. All their religious enthusiasm led them into a dead end of despair and spiritual darkness.

If you want to find a definition of a negative identity, it is right here!

## Transformation

But the verses of Ephesians 2:13–15 offer a turning point:

But now in Christ Jesus you who once were far away have been brought near by the blood of Christ.

For he himself is our peace, who has made the two groups one and has destroyed the barrier, the dividing wall of hostility, by setting aside in his flesh the law with its commands and regulations. His purpose was to create in himself one new humanity out of the two, thus making peace . . .

The blessings promised to Israel have come to the Gentiles through Christ and his death on the cross. In an obvious reference to the wall in the temple, Paul says that Jesus destroyed the dividing wall of hostility. The death of Jesus has changed everything.

The Gospels record what happened at the moment of his death:

> And when Jesus had cried out again in a loud voice, he gave up his spirit. At that moment the curtain of the temple was torn in two from top to bottom.
> (Matthew 27:50–51)

The tearing of the curtain showed that access to God was now open, by the blood of Jesus. But it also represented the abolition of the old religion of exclusion. Gentiles can now enjoy friendship with God and fellowship with everyone else who has been reconciled to God through Jesus.

It is the cross that achieves this. God brings us in through the blood of Christ (2:13), abolishing the barrier through his flesh, torn on the cross for us (2:15). He reconciles us through the cross (2:16). The ground before the cross is level. Whatever our social, racial or national background, we come to God in the same way. He delights in every one of his children with an equal intensity.

This is what our nameless African politician discovered. God sent Philip the evangelist to meet him on his homeward journey. While in Jerusalem, the man had bought a copy of the prophecy of Isaiah and was reading the prophet's prediction of the death of Christ:

> he was led like a sheep to the slaughter,
>     and as a lamb before its shearer is silent,
>     so he did not open his mouth.
> (Isaiah 53:7; Acts 8:32)

Philip explained the meaning of the passage to him: 'Then Philip began with that very passage of Scripture and told him the good news about Jesus' (Acts 8:35).

The man was baptized and went on his way, rejoicing. He had become part of the new humanity whose people were reconciled to God and to one another through the cross of Christ.

He belonged.

## Reconciliation

Paul now makes a most remarkable statement:

and in one body to reconcile both of them to God through the cross, by which he put to death their hostility. He came and preached peace to you who were far away and peace to those who were near.
(Ephesians 2:16–17)

God has created a new humanity – one body made up of everyone who believes. Christians have become the third race. They are no longer referred to as Jews or Gentiles, but as something else.

My identity supersedes the 'accidents' of my birth. I still support the England football team and I am proud to be a Brummie (a person from the city of Birmingham). These things clearly contribute to my identity and influence the person that I am. But there is now something deeper. By grace I have become a member of the new humanity. This is what now defines me more than my national or cultural experience.

In the early church, differences between Jews and Gentiles persisted. Often manifested in the celebration of certain days or in scruples about diet, these had to be carefully managed. But the apostles do not insist that new converts abandon their former culture. Diversity of cultural experience is to be celebrated within the context of mutual respect and love.

One of the richest experiences I enjoy is that of preaching in different cultural contexts. I can think of an Asian church in Birmingham where I used to speak at a gathering for men. Timing is relaxed, but the evening is always filled with singing in Urdu, prayer, more singing, a Bible message conveyed with the help of an interpreter, more singing, a curry, more singing, a second message (the first time I went, no one warned me that I would be expected to speak twice!), more singing, prayer and, just to finish, more singing. It is culturally a million miles away from my own church experience, but there is an instant sense of connection. I know I am among my brothers.

Belonging to the new humanity supersedes all secondary cultural commitments.

## Living for others

Many books on identity ignore this dimension of the subject. Identity merely becomes a quest for personal fulfilment. But what Paul says here makes this impossible. I can only discover my true identity as I kneel with all my brothers and sisters at the foot of the cross and rejoice that God has now brought me into a new family. I cannot be reconciled to God without being reconciled to my brothers and sisters.

The cross destroys the hostility that once existed. It supersedes everything that had gone before. Listen to Paul elsewhere:

Therefore, if anyone is in Christ, the new creation has come: the old has gone, the new is here!
(2 Corinthians 5:17)

There is neither Jew nor Gentile, neither slave nor free, nor is there male and female, for you are all one in Christ Jesus.
(Galatians 3:28)

In the body of Christ, all racial and ethnic divisions are absent. The cross brings us together. As we gaze at the cross, we are overwhelmed with God's grace towards us and lay down the weapons of our hostility towards him and one another.

I find my identity within this new humanity. Ironically, it comes from loving myself less and loving Christ and other people more: 'And he died for all, that those who live should no longer live for themselves but for him who died for them and was raised again' (2 Corinthians 5:15).

Paul describes this kind of life in Colossians 3:12–14:

> Therefore, as God's chosen people, holy and dearly loved, clothe yourselves with compassion, kindness, humility, gentleness and patience. Bear with each other and forgive one another if any of you has a grievance against someone. Forgive as the Lord forgave you. And over all these virtues put on love, which binds them all together in perfect unity.

We are 'God's chosen people, holy and dearly loved'. If this is who we are, it must shape our behaviour. Paul uses the metaphor of wearing a uniform. Just as you would recognize a soldier or a police officer by their uniform, so you should recognize a Christian by the way they are clothed. What is the uniform? It is compassion, kindness, humility, gentleness, patience, forgiveness and love!

This is a description of a life lived not for self, but for others. Because we have been loved and cherished and have experienced the servant-heartedness of Jesus, we must love, cherish and serve one another.

Being part of the new humanity is incredible and wonderful but it carries with it the duty to live like this.

Paul has not finished yet.

## A new intimacy

As members of a new family, we now have an intimate relationship with the triune God: 'For through him we both have access to the Father by one Spirit (Ephesians 2:18).

Prayer draws us into the eternal loving relationship of the Trinity. We come to the Father, through the Son, in the power of the Holy Spirit. Even Jewish believers were kept at a distance in the Jerusalem Temple. Only the High Priest could enter the Holy of Holies and, even then, only once a year. But now all Christians – whether formerly Jews or Gentiles – have a new closeness to God.

70

We come into the presence of the Father, where we find grace to nourish us, protect us and uphold us. He is now our Father who is in heaven, and his throne is a throne of grace.

We come through Christ. He reconciles us to the Father and presents us faultless in his presence. He pleads for us when we are weak, defends us when we are attacked and seeks mercy for us when we stumble.

We come by the power and prompting of the Holy Spirit. He teaches us to pray and takes our weak efforts, making them intelligible and pleasing to God.

You will notice that we come together. Personal prayer is essential, but so too is corporate prayer. As we draw near to God, we draw near to one another. Just as the spokes of a bicycle wheel get closer as they reach the centre of the wheel, so we get closer to one another as we get closer to God.

## A new temple

Finally, we reach the climax of the passage:

> Consequently, you are no longer foreigners and strangers, but fellow citizens with God's people and also members of his household, built on the foundation of the apostles and prophets, with Christ Jesus himself as the chief cornerstone. In him the whole building is joined together and rises to become a holy temple in the Lord. And in him you too are being built together to become a dwelling in which God lives by his Spirit.
> (Ephesians 2:19–22)

Paul gives us three magnificent pictures of the church.

### • A kingdom in which we have become citizens
As I write, there are images on the news of stateless refugees willing to risk their lives in leaky makeshift boats. We may look at their haunted faces and wonder why. The answer is that they are seeking

citizenship in a place where they and their families can experience a fuller life. The death of Jesus has made us citizens of the kingdom of God. My identity is defined by my citizenship of this kingdom and my allegiance to its king.

### • A family or household

Those who were once outside the intimate circle of the home have now been brought into the family (2:19; Matthew 12:49–50). We have God as our Father, Christ as our older brother and all other believers as our siblings. We have a place at the table. Every time we take bread and wine, we are celebrating the fact that we belong.

### • A spiritual temple

Since Pentecost, God no longer manifests his glory in a physical building. He now dwells in the lives of individual Christians (1 Corinthians 6:19–20) and in the church. Each one of us is a spiritual stone. We are being built together into the place where God is pleased to dwell. The stones come in a variety of shapes and sizes, but they all belong and they are all needed.

The church is to be an inclusive, welcoming community where we are called together to be a people of love and mutual support.

Can you see how impossible it is to try to work out our identity in glorious isolation? We sometimes think that self-reliance is a sign of maturity. Nothing is further from the truth. We must resist the individualism that pervades the church, especially in the West. We need to learn to be vulnerable with one another. There is an African proverb: 'If you want to go fast, go alone; If you want to go far, go together'. We are not supposed to go it alone.

## Communities of grace

Our identity can only be worked out in community. So much of the nitty-gritty of how we experience love, forgiveness and grace is worked out through, and experienced within, the relationships of our Christian community. It's in our fellowship groups or with our prayer partners or our friendship networks that this happens. Here we have a chance to speak honestly about our struggles and sin – and to know that we are loved and forgiven. It's only because we are assured of our identity and forgiveness in Christ that we can speak openly and appropriately with other Christians, bear one another's burdens and know encouragement and growth. This relational component marks out the relationships we have within the church family and provides a community of grace where we can become the people God wants us to be.

Church can be a bit messy. Sometimes it is tempting to opt out, but if we take the Bible seriously, we will see that this option is not open to us. For all its imperfections, the church is the foretaste of the harmony that God will one day bring to the whole of creation. God draws attention to the church as the present demonstration of his future plans – just like a movie trailer!

Moviemakers put lots of money into creating movie trailers because a good trailer will whet your appetite and make you want to see the film.

If people visited your church and 'saw the trailer', would they want to see the movie too?

## Questions

1 Why do we want to belong? What happens to us when we feel excluded?

2 How do we build walls of exclusion in the church? Why are they wrong? What should we do about them?

3 We all bring our cultural experience to the church. How can this have a positive effect? How can it lead to a negative outcome?

4 Look at Acts 2:42–47 and Hebrews 10:24–25. What are the practical implications of belonging to the church?

5 How should the church be a realistic foretaste of the unity that Christ will one day establish in the new heavens and the new earth?

# 6

# Everyone is needed

## Ephesians 4:1–16

### Moses' mother

One hot Saturday evening in a small church in Wales, as an eleven-year-old, I heard the call to come to Christ. With a joy that I cannot describe, I 'fled to the cross'. The call was clear and compelling, and becoming a Christian has remained the greatest event in my life.

Many Christians cannot point to a specific moment, but they know that God has called them to himself. This decisive call to salvation is part of our God-given identity (Romans 8:28–30). We have been called out of darkness into God's wonderful light (1 Peter 2:9), called to eternal life, peace, fellowship and freedom. All these phrases are descriptions of what it means to be a Christian and apply to every believer. They describe what we are, rather than what we do. They never change and they form the bedrock of our identity.

This is the primary way in which the Bible uses the word 'calling'. There is a secondary use of the word too, which refers to what we do rather than what we are.

By the time I was fourteen, I knew that I wanted to dedicate my life to Christian ministry.

As I progressed through my teens, the sense of calling never went away. It shaped my choices and moulded my outlook. After studying theology and spending five years as a teacher, I was called into pastoral ministry at the age of twenty-six. For nearly four decades now, I have had the inestimable privilege of being a pastor. Every day, I get to pray and study God's word. Two or three times a week, I preach. I have the opportunity to counsel God's people or share the gospel with men and women who don't know Jesus. From time to time, I attend meetings where I encourage and am encouraged by other pastors, and I have the chance to commit to writing some of the amazing truths with which God has nourished my soul. This is my day job too!

Being in ministry is like being the mother of Moses: she got to care for her infant son – and was paid for it (Exodus 2:1–10).

In this secondary sense of the word, the ministry has been my 'calling'.

## Identity and calling

Every Christian has a calling of this secondary sort.

Discipleship implies that we submit to the lordship of Christ in everything we do. This crosses the unbiblical secular/sacred divide that we sometimes impose on our lives. So, Paul tells slaves to see their service for their earthly masters as part of their service for Christ: 'Serve wholeheartedly, as if you were serving the Lord, not people, because you know that the Lord will reward each one for whatever good they do, whether they are slave or free' (Ephesians 6:7–8).

We live in a very different world today, one that recognizes the evil of slavery. William Wilberforce opposed slavery in the nineteenth century and Christians are still at the forefront of the battle against modern-day 'slavery' in its various forms. However, the underlying principle still holds true. Our Christian faith should mould our attitude in everything we do, including our daily work. We are to serve diligently, as if we are serving the Lord. Whatever our calling, we are to fulfil it with enthusiasm, honesty and sincerity, because our work is part of our Christian discipleship.

'Full-time Christian ministry' is not superior to every other calling or profession in life. If we take seriously the principles of whole-life discipleship, we will come to recognize that everything we do is for the glory of God (1 Corinthians 10:31). We have also been called to serve God within the local church. Paul addresses this in Ephesians 4, as we will explore below. We must not, however, confine our understanding of this subject to what we do in church.

Whatever job I do as a Christian, it is a holy calling from God. 'Secular' work is not second rate or of little value. My job is not just the means I use to keep the wolf from the door so that I can do the real work – the work that counts – serving God in his church. This is an unbiblical dichotomy. We speak of people who are in 'full-time ministry' as if only they are 'full-time Christians'. We are all full-time Christians, wherever God has put us. We should never devalue our work or retreat into a constant round of church meetings that become the real focus of our lives and passions.

In this way, I can legitimately refer to my work – in church or in the world – as my 'calling', but it is always the secondary calling. It is what I do rather than what I am. What I am, my status with God, can never change. What I do, my service for God, may change over my lifetime. My secondary calling matters, but only because the primary calling matters most. We must hold these two together but ensure that they are kept in the right order.

With this in mind, we will turn to Ephesians 4 and explore what Paul has to say about our calling to serve God in the local church.

## Cut and thrust in the local church

Something very significant happens in Ephesians 4:1.

Up to this point, Paul has been describing the treasures that we have in Christ. God has blessed us in him with every spiritual blessing in the heavenly realm. He concludes with a glorious doxology:

> Now to him who is able to do immeasurably more than all we ask or imagine, according to his power that is at work within us, to him be glory in the church and in Christ Jesus throughout all generations, for ever and ever! Amen.
> (Ephesians 3:20–21)

We move now from belief to behaviour. Paul directs Christians to live a life worthy of all the blessings described in the first three

77

chapters of Ephesians. He applies this to the church, the world, the home and the workplace.

Paul begins by describing the way in which we should relate to one another within the church. The church is a foretaste of the unity that will one day exist in the universe when it is united under the lordship of Christ (3:10–11). It is important that the church displays this unity now. Unity is a gift of God, since he is the one who creates it (2:14), but we must work hard to maintain it.

> As a prisoner for the Lord, then, I urge you to live a life worthy of the calling you have received. Be completely humble and gentle; be patient, bearing with one another in love. Make every effort to keep the unity of the Spirit through the bond of peace. There is one body and one Spirit, just as you were called to one hope when you were called; one Lord, one faith, one baptism; one God and Father of all, who is over all and through all and in all.
> (Ephesians 4:1–6)

We must guard our hearts and be both humble and gentle.

Humility is an attitude of lowliness, the opposite of pride. Gentleness is a mildness of character that refuses to insist on its own way. It is not spineless, but it does seek the good of others. It leads to patience and forbearance.

Paul also reminds the Ephesians of the foundations on which the unity of the church is built (4:4–6). At conversion, we were all baptized into the one Body of Christ. We share one hope and we will spend eternity together. We confess one faith. Our unity is based on our relationship with the triune God: one Father, one Lord (Jesus) and one Spirit.

## Unity, not uniformity

God has given unity to his church as a gift, but what will it look like? Does it mean that we will all be identical in our experiences, gifts and Christian service? Are Christians just clones with no variety, diversity or variability?

Unity is important, but it is not uniformity.

At school, I made friends with a boy who was a Jehovah's Witness. He invited me to attend the Kingdom Hall, where his family worshipped. I agreed, on condition that he would also attend my church.

The meeting was friendly but slightly bizarre because the message was delivered from a reel-to-reel tape recorder. We sat listening to a disembodied voice speaking from John 5, on the healing of the lame man. I remember nothing of the content, but what I do recall was the conversation we had afterwards. My friend told me that every Kingdom Hall in the UK would be hearing the same message that Sunday, and he boasted, 'We Witnesses are all taught the same things and we believe exactly the same truths.'

At the time, I thought it was a bit spooky. Since then, my conclusions have been confirmed. He didn't ever come to my church, but he got me thinking about the wonderful diversity that exists among true Bible-believing Christians.

Of course, there are basic Christian truths about which every true believer will be convinced, but unity is not the same as bland and programmed uniformity. God loves diversity.

Paul addresses this in Ephesians 4:7-16:

But to each one of us grace has been given as Christ apportioned it. This is why it says:

'When he ascended on high,
  he took many captives
  and gave gifts to his people.'

(What does 'he ascended' mean except that he also descended to the lower, earthly regions? He who descended is the very one who ascended higher than all the heavens, in order to fill the whole universe.) So Christ himself gave the apostles, the prophets, the evangelists, the pastors and teachers, to equip

79

his people for works of service, so that the body of Christ may be built up until we all reach unity in the faith and in the knowledge of the Son of God and become mature, attaining to the whole measure of the fullness of Christ.

Then we will no longer be infants, tossed back and forth by the waves, and blown here and there by every wind of teaching and by the cunning and craftiness of people in their deceitful scheming. Instead, speaking the truth in love, we will grow to become in every respect the mature body of him who is the head, that is, Christ. From him the whole body, joined and held together by every supporting ligament, grows and builds itself up in love, as each part does its work.

The church is a body with many parts, each of them fulfilling their God-given, unique function. Each of us is to be committed to the church and to use our spiritual gifts for its good.

## Spiritual gifts

The Hawthorns is the highest football ground in England. At 552 feet (168 metres) above sea level, it is just ahead of Boundary Park (Oldham Athletic FC) and Vale Park (Port Vale FC). It's not high enough to get a nosebleed but high enough to boast about when there is little else to warm the heart of a West Bromwich Albion supporter!

What is it like to go to a match? You pay your money and find your seat. You chat to the people around you, then watch the performance on the pitch. You sing and eat a pie at half time. You sing again and then go home. On the way home, you may well comment on the performance of the professionals. The result may affect your mood for a couple of days, and you may think about your team in the week.

If you replace the pies with coffee and biscuits, it sounds a lot like church.

For many people, church is a spectator sport. We slip in, slump down, sing up and then slip out again. At a football match, we may be highly critical of the performance of our team, but we know that our place is on the terraces, watching the professionals in action. In church, we take a similarly passive role. Church is a weekly event in which minimum participation is required.

This is an unhealthy aberration.

In this section, Paul lays down the biblical pattern of an all-member ministry. Discovering our role within the local church contributes significantly to our identity.

## Paul's five principles

### 1 Every Christian has a spiritual gift

A gift is a capacity for service, given to every Christian without exception for the good of the body of Christ. We have at least one gift (4:7). No one has all the gifts, but there is no such thing as a gift-less Christian.

Elsewhere Paul says, 'Now to each one the manifestation of the Spirit is given for the common good' (1 Corinthians 12:7).

There are five lists of gifts (Romans 12:6-8; 1 Corinthians 12:8-10; 12:28-30; Ephesians 4:11-12; 1 Peter 4:10-11). These lists are not intended to be comprehensive but testify to the wonderful diversity that exists in the church. They can be dramatic or comparatively mundane, but every Christian will have at least one.

To identify our gifts, we need to ask ourselves several questions.

- What are my natural capacities?
- What do I enjoy doing?
- What do my circumstances or experiences enable me to do?
- What do I get excited about?
- What seems to bear good fruit?
- What do mature Christians, who know me well, think?

### 2 The gifts come from Jesus

Paul tells us three times that the gifts have been given directly by Jesus (Ephesians 4:7, 8, 11). When Jesus ascended to heaven, he defeated his enemies and, like a mighty conqueror, distributed gifts to his followers (Ephesians 4:8–10; Psalm 68:18). The ascended Christ gave the Holy Spirit to the church, and with him comes spiritual gifts (Acts 2:33).

Two points follow from this.

If the gifts are given by Christ, we cannot boast about them. Pride is a perennial problem in the church. It is easy for us to feel superior to others because of the gifts we have, or to feel slighted when our gifts are not recognized. We need to work hard to hone and refine our service, but every gift comes from Christ and there is no room for boasting.

Another mistake is to despise our gifts and to downplay their importance. We often think that this is a sign of humility, but it isn't. If they come from the hands of Jesus, they are valuable and must never be treated with contempt. We are called to use them, not to hide or deride them (Matthew 25:14–30).

### 3 Gifts include the gift of leadership

The four gifts that Paul identifies in 4:11 are leadership gifts.

When God wants to bless his people, he sends them good and godly leaders. Leadership is vital to the health of the church and to the fulfilment of its mission.

Jesus invested much of his time in training the apostles. After Pentecost, the apostles give clear and courageous leadership to the young church. Christian missionaries made sure that every new church had a healthy leadership team in place (Acts 14:23; Titus 1:5). Paul invested a lot of time in training and preparing a new generation of leaders and was concerned that the leaders he trained should share his vision (2 Timothy 2:2).

The first two gifts mentioned here – apostles and prophets – are foundational (Ephesians 2:20; 3:5). The evangelist is a messenger of good news, who presents the gospel in a biblically faithful and culturally relevant way. A pastor-teacher describes one gift or ministry: the gift involves leading the flock (shepherding) and feeding the sheep (teaching).

Leaders are called to lead, but they are to do so with gentleness, humility and restraint. One of the problems in some churches is dictatorial leadership. I have encountered situations in which leadership has become abusive and harmful. We are called to treat our leaders with respect but never to surrender our consciences to them.

At the root of abusive leadership, there is often an identity problem. Leaders who are comfortable about their identity in Christ are less likely to be abusive. Toxic leadership often flows from insecurity. If our leadership, rather than Christ, becomes the principal ingredient in our identity then we may react in an overbearing way when we feel that it is being challenged. The antidote is to make sure that my identity is built on Jesus and not on the gifts he has given me.

## 4 The job of leaders is to mobilize the flock

What are leaders for? What is their job description? The key lies in Paul's words in Ephesians 4:12.

- Leaders are to equip God's people. The word 'equip' can be used for mending nets (Matthew 4:21). It means to restore, complete and enable. Leaders are to mend the nets of our service potential so that we can be more effective.
- Leaders are to do the above so that God's people can do works of service. They help God's people to recognize and use their gifts both within the church and within the workplace, neighbourhood and beyond. All God's people are to be involved in sharing the gospel (1 Peter 3:15) and encouraging one another (Hebrews 10:24–25).
- The result of this leadership is that the body of Christ will be built up and grow towards maturity. This is the opposite of one-man-band ministry. If leaders try to control everything and refuse to equip and mobilize others, then the church will be paralyzed and petrified.

Paul clearly acknowledges the importance of leadership, but the leader is there to mobilize God's people. Christianity is not a spectator sport. It is not the realm of the professionals, where the layperson simply watches and supports the ministry of the experts.

Moses learned this from his father-in-law Jethro (Exodus 18), and Nehemiah applied the principle when rebuilding the walls of Jerusalem (Nehemiah 3). When people are mobilized, ministries are multiplied, gifts are developed and the work of the church flourishes.

## 5 This is the only the way to reach maturity

When the church operates like this, there will be unity in relationship, progress in knowledge and growing in maturity (Ephesians 4:13). Christians are no longer led astray by false teaching but speak the truth in love (4:14–15). Paul ends with a description of a healthy church: 'From him the whole body, joined and held together by every supporting ligament, grows and builds itself up in love, as each part does its work' (4:16).

Here is the church as it is meant to be, marked out by the unity of faith, the stability of truth and the security of love.

# Identity and service

What has this got to do with identity?

It seems to me that there are two dangers to avoid.

On the one hand, we need to avoid the temptation of defining our identity by what we do rather than what we are in Christ. It is tempting to do this because of the energy, time and emotional commitment that we often give to our career or our service. If the first answer to the question 'Who am I?' is 'I am a teacher' or 'I am a mechanic' or 'I am a pastor' or 'I am a home group leader', we are in danger of understanding our identity in the wrong terms. The problem is that, with a job or a ministry as the key to understanding my identity, the emphasis is in the wrong place. I can easily turn my work or service into an idol. It is also a transitory thing – I may be a teacher now, but one day I will retire. What happens to my identity then? I have met many people who are bitter or confused or frustrated because they have defined themselves by what they do rather than what they are.

On the other hand, it is dangerous to divorce our identity from our work entirely. What we do is important. It may not define us, but it does become an important ingredient in our self-understanding. There is great dignity in work. God himself is a worker who delights in the magnificence of the creation and the wonders of new creation. He calls us, as creatures made in his image, to delight in the work of our hands. We are all called to serve him by using the spiritual gifts Christ has given us. If I sit on my hands, I will miss the purpose for which God joined me to the Body of Christ. I will suffer, but so too will my brothers and sisters.

## What next?

I love being a pastor. I cannot imagine doing anything else.

There lies the the rub. At this stage in my life, I need to begin to think about retirement. When will it happen? What will it look like? What will I spend my time doing?

I remember the first day of my ministry. It was Monday 2 August 1982. In the morning, I began to study for a sermon on trials and temptations from James 1:1–8. In the afternoon, I spent some time with one of our mission partners, who was back in the UK for a well-deserved rest. In the evening, I met with a couple of my elders and we prayed about the direction of the church.

Those are very vivid memories.

What will the last day of my ministry feel like? Is there life after ministry?! Ministry has played such a crucial part in forming my identity. So, what happens when I am no longer a minister?

Here is the problem: our identity is inevitably tied up with a whole series of clearly defined roles. I am a minister; I am a son and a brother; I am a husband; I am a dad and a grandad.

But what happens when I can no longer define myself in those ways?

I had an insight into this when, ten years into my ministry, my wife became desperately ill. We had three children and another one on the way. I had to face the very real possibility that I would have to step out of ministry and become a full-time carer. I love my wife and would count it a privilege to serve her in this way, but the thought of never preaching again devastated me. I wrestled with

God over it and he won. I came to the point of submission, where I was willing to relinquish my ministry and find my satisfaction and identity in Christ alone.

I did not have to step down, although my wife's ongoing incapacity has set limits. I love my job, but I do not worship it. I know that it is a gift from God and it would be churlish to fail to delight in the gift. However, when my full-time ministry ends, I have something much more precious and far more satisfying to delight in. I have something eternal and unchangeable. I have Christ.

He is the one thing in my life that can always be relied on never to change.

## Questions

1 What do the following verses teach us about our calling as Christians: Galatians 5:13; Colossians 3:15; 1 Thessalonians 4:7; and 1 Peter 2:20–21; 3:9?
2 We are all 'full-time' Christians. How should this affect my attitude to my work, rest and play?
3 Do you know what your spiritual gifts are? How would you go about finding out? Are you using them?
4 Why is good leadership necessary in the local church?
5 How is my identity related to my career or service for Christ?

# 7

# Everyone worships something

## Ephesians 5:18–21

### Close encounters

My daughter Keziah was three years old when she fell in love with elephants.

After we had shown her Disney's *Dumbo*, everything was about elephants. We had elephant pictures on the wall, elephant soft toys in the toybox and every bedtime story had to be about elephants. You get the picture!

So, we took her to the zoo to see the real thing.

Excitement mounted as we passed a whole menagerie of lesser species. Forget the lions and bears and monkeys – all she really wanted to see were the elephants. When we got to their enclosure there was a crowd obscuring our vision. We could smell them before we could see them. Eventually we managed to work our way to the front of the crowd. Just as we turned Keziah's pushchair in his direction, one of the big beasts obligingly came towards us and bent his head downwards to where his greatest fan was breathlessly waiting.

So, Keziah came face to face with an elephant for the first time.

I will never forget her reaction. As she stared up at this towering pachyderm, her jaw dropped, her eyes grew wide and with a mixture of wonder, joy and not a little fear, she exclaimed, 'Oh wow!'

Meeting an elephant in the flesh is very different from watching a cartoon or cuddling a soft toy. For a three-year-old it is a never-to-be-forgotten encounter with something much bigger than she can ever possibly imagine.

# Enter Job

Whenever I think of that, I am reminded of Job's encounter with the living God.

After walking the most painful road of suffering imaginable, Job finally meets the Lord:

> Then the LORD spoke to Job out of the storm. He said:

> Who is this that obscures my plans
> with words without knowledge?
> Brace yourself like a man;
> I will question you,
> and you shall answer me.
> (Job 38:1–3)

God draws back the veil that hides his glory. At the end of the encounter, Job is a changed man:

> I know that you can do all things;
> no purpose of yours can be thwarted.
> You asked, 'Who is this that obscures my plans
> with words without knowledge?'
> Surely I spoke of things I did not understand,
> things too wonderful for me to know.

> You said, 'Listen now, and I will speak;
> I will question you,
> and you shall answer me.'
> My ears had heard of you
> but now my eyes have seen you.
> Therefore I despise myself
> and repent in dust and ashes.
> (Job 42:2–6)

You can study the doctrine of God, read books about him, hear sermons that extol his greatness, but everything changes when you meet him. The only appropriate response in such circumstances is, 'Oh wow!'

We have a far too domesticated view of God. Whenever people encounter God in the Bible, they are overwhelmed by his majesty and overcome by his glory. They experience what Rudolf Otto called 'Mysterium tremendum et fascinans'.[1] You do not have to know Latin to work this one out. The God we meet in the pages of Scripture is mysterious (*mysterium*), awesome (*tremendum*) and fascinating (*fascinans*), all at the same time.

This is why worship is at the centre of my understanding of my identity.

Who am I? I am a worshipper. And what I worship determines my identity.

## 24/7 worship

Worship is the total response of all that I am to all that God has revealed of himself to me. When the Bible speaks of worship, it seems to have two closely related reference points.

One broader definition sees worship as covering the totality of life. It is the 24/7 response of my whole life to God. I worship God in everything I do – from cooking a meal to cutting the lawn; from reading a book to changing a tyre; from kissing my wife to running a marathon.

This is what Paul has in mind in Romans 12:1–2:

> Therefore, I urge you, brothers and sisters, in view of God's mercy, to offer your bodies as a living sacrifice, holy and pleasing to God – this is your true and proper worship. Do not conform to the pattern of this world but be transformed by the renewing of your mind. Then you will be able to test and approve what God's will is – his good, pleasing and perfect will.

To be a living sacrifice is to recognize that there is not a corner of my life that does not belong to God. The purpose of my existence is to discover his will and to do it. My highest motive is to please him.

Clearly, this has huge implications for my self-understanding and my identity. I cannot live my life as if my own pleasure or even the pleasure of others were my primary goal or purpose. I live for God. Listen to how Patrick Collinson describes the Puritans:

> The life of the Puritan was in one sense a continuous act of worship, pursued under an unremitting and lively sense of God's providential purposes and constantly refreshed by religious activity, personal, domestic and public.[2]

This is what whole-life worship looks like.

## Declaring God's praise

There is a second way in which the Bible refers to worship, a kind of subset of the first definition, but one that merits separate treatment as a distinctive Christian exercise. It relates to those specific times when Christians seek to bring praise to God and delight in his character. It involves the verbalization of our love, adoration and godly fear. In worship we come to know his glory and to confess his greatness. We praise his name and declare his majesty. We sing his praises and surrender to his will. We behold him and become like him.

The definition by former Archbishop of Canterbury, William Temple, is well known:

> Worship is the submission of all of our nature to God. It is the quickening of the conscience by his holiness; the nourishment of mind with his truth; the purifying of imagination by his beauty; the opening of the heart to his love; the surrender of will to his purpose – all this gathered up in adoration, the most selfless emotion of which our nature is capable.[3]

Such worship is fed by Scripture, empowered by the Holy Spirit and focused on Christ. It is vital to our self-understanding and our true identity as Christians.

## The gravitational pull of self-obsession

One of the key challenges that we face when we think about identity is the danger of self-obsession. The media screams at us that we need to love ourselves and the basic problem at the heart of our lives is lack of self-worth and self-acceptance. We need to look in the mirror each morning and repeat to ourselves, 'I love me. I am wonderful. I am the best thing that has ever happened to me.'

Now, that sounds very much like worship! In this case, we have replaced God with ourselves. We have succumbed to idolatry. We can even turn God's grace on its head. Why did God rescue me? Because I am worth it! This proves that I am precious – he could not do without me!

But this is not what the Bible teaches. The grace of God rescues rebels and the reason for grace lies in his character, not in my worthiness. I was worthy of judgment, not mercy! Of course, God loves me – he gave his Son to rescue me. I am precious to God, but this is not because of my intrinsic worth. It is because his grace has brought me into his family.

How can I guard my heart against idolatry? How can I resist the gravitational pull of self-obsession?

The answer lies in worship. When I deliberately turn my mind away from myself and am lost in the magnificence of God, the focus has to change. I can say, 'I love you. You are wonderful. You are the best thing that has ever happened to me.'

This is why worship is so vital to my identity. Worship is about what we love and live for. We turn to idols because we imagine that they will bring us joy and protection. Yet, only God can give us real joy or provide the unshakeable foundation on which to build our lives. Worship acts as a kind of emetic, flushing out the self-obsession that poisons our lives.

## The greatness of God

Worship is a contentious area and we often hear of 'worship wars' – what do we sing, how do we sing it and who leads the singing? But the real worship war is in my heart. I have to fight against the constant desire to dethrone God and put something else in his place. I must be relentless in my pursuit of God and his glory. I can only know myself as I know him, and I can only really know him as I bow in adoration at his feet.

Listen to veteran theologian Jim Packer:

> Today, vast stress is laid on the thought that God is personal, but this truth is so stated as to leave the impression that God is a person of the same sort as we are – weak, inadequate, ineffective, a little pathetic. But this is not the God of the Bible! Our personal life is a finite thing: it is limited in every direction, in space, in time, in knowledge, in power. But God is not so limited. He is eternal, infinite and almighty. He has us in his hands; we never have him in ours. Like us, he is personal; but unlike us, he is great.[4]

God is great and greatly to be praised. We are to approach him with adoring joy and reverent fear. He may be my friend, but he is not my mate.

We can only approach the Father through the Son. The writer to the Hebrews gives us this compelling invitation:

> Therefore, brothers and sisters, since we have confidence to enter the Most Holy Place by the blood of Jesus, by a new and living way opened for us through the curtain, that is, his body, and since we have a great priest over the house of God, let us draw near to God with a sincere heart and with the full assurance that faith brings, having our hearts sprinkled to cleanse us from a guilty conscience and having our bodies washed with pure water.
> (Hebrews 10:19–22)

By his death, Jesus opened the way into God's presence. He takes us by the hand, brings us into God's presence and gives us access to God's grace. There is no worship without the cross. Listen to the song of heaven:

You are worthy to take the scroll
　and to open its seals,
because you were slain,
　and with your blood you purchased for God
　persons from every tribe and language and people
　　and nation.
You have made them to be a kingdom and priests
　　to serve our God,
　and they will reign on the earth.
(Revelation 5:9–10)

We can only come in the power of the Holy Spirit. He is the one who illuminates our minds with the truth he has revealed in Scripture. With this truth, he warms our emotions so that we begin to love Christ. This, in turn, will shape our wills and change the direction of our lives.

So, Christian worship is Trinitarian: 'For through him (Jesus Christ) we both have access to the Father by one Spirit' (Ephesians 2:18).

## The work of the Holy Spirit

All of us worship something. It is built into our personalities and my identity is shaped by what I worship. The longer I spend in God's presence, the more I come to understand his character. As I contemplate the love and mercy that reach down to wretches like me, the more I will be transformed into his likeness.

When Moses spent time in God's presence on Mount Sinai, it showed in his face. The glory of God was reflected. As we spend time – corporately or individually – in God's presence, we too will come to display this transformation of character.

Now the Lord is the Spirit, and where the Spirit of the Lord is, there is freedom. And we all, who with unveiled faces contemplate the Lord's glory, are being transformed into his image

with ever-increasing glory, which comes from the Lord, who is the Spirit.
(2 Corinthians 3:17–18)

Paul addresses the subject of worship in Ephesians 5:18–21:

> Do not get drunk on wine, which leads to debauchery. Instead, be filled with the Spirit, speaking to one another with psalms, hymns, and songs from the Spirit. Sing and make music from your heart to the Lord, always giving thanks to God the Father for everything, in the name of our Lord Jesus Christ. Submit to one another out of reverence for Christ.

Paul is teaching about the Spirit-filled life. The Spirit enables us to grow into our true identity, so that we become like Christ. It is through the Spirit that the purpose of complete renovation takes place.

Paul has already told the Christians in Ephesus that they have been sealed with the Spirit (1:13–14). The sealing confirms and shapes our new identity. In Ephesians 5:18, he commands them to be filled with the Spirit. All Christians have the Spirit (1:13–14; Acts 2:16–17, 38–39), but not all are filled with the Spirit, hence the command.

Notice the contrast with drunkenness. Perhaps this was a particular problem in pagan Ephesus – the worship of Dionysius often led to drunken orgies. However, Paul is also contrasting drunkenness with the filling of the Spirit. Drunken people are 'controlled' by the influence of the alcohol in their bloodstream. It affects the way that they walk, talk, think and act. It is visible and obvious.

The same should be true of the people who are filled with the Spirit. He controls their inner thoughts and outward actions. But whereas alcohol depresses the brain, the Spirit is the great stimulant who inspires us to love Christ and to desire to be like him. Excessive alcohol removes our inhibitions and often provokes sinful actions; the Spirit raises our desire for holiness and enables us to realize our new identity in Christ. Intoxication dehumanizes us, whereas the Spirit makes us more like Christ, the perfect model of true humanity.

## The Spirit-filled life

To understand the above command, we need to break it down.

It is an *imperative* or instruction, that is, not a hint, polite suggestion or a nice idea, but a clear command. Commands are not to be debated but obeyed. If we neglect to follow the command, it is tantamount to disobedience.

It is *plural* – for all Christians. It is not a kind of second-level experience for particularly mature Christians. It is not confined to ministers or missionaries or Christian 'celebrities'. The Spirit-filled life is the normal Christian life.

It is *passive* – God does it for us. It is not a human achievement. We are to work out our salvation with fear and trembling, but we do so always conscious that it is God who gives us both the desire and the ability to live such a life (Philippians 2:12–13). Living a Spirit-filled life means walking in dependence on God. Jesus promised to give the Spirit to those who ask in humble, childlike faith (Luke 11:9–13).

It is in the *present continuous tense* – literally, *'be being filled'*. It is an ongoing experience, not a once-for-all-time event. Each day, I come to God, the source of abundant grace, and ask him to fill me afresh with his Spirit. There is no limit to the number of times we can ask and no limit to the number of times God will fill us.

There is a well-known story about C. H. Spurgeon, the nineteenth-century Baptist minister we met in chapter 1. He was riding home one evening after a heavy day's work. He felt weary and depressed. Suddenly he remembered 2 Corinthians 12:9: 'My grace is sufficient for thee.' As he thought about this, he was overwhelmed with joy and humbled that he had forgotten such a vital truth. To doubt God's sufficiency was absurd:

It was as though some little fish, being very thirsty, was troubled about drinking the river dry, and the river said, 'Drink away, little fish, my stream is sufficient for thee.' Or, it seemed after the seven years of plenty, a mouse feared that it would die of famine, and Joseph might say, 'Cheer up, little mouse, my granaries are sufficient for thee.' Or, a man away up on a mountain saying to himself, 'I fear I shall exhaust all the oxygen in the atmosphere.' But the earth might say, 'Breathe away, oh man, and fill thy lungs ever; my atmosphere is sufficient for thee.' Little faith will bring our souls to Heaven, but great faith will bring Heaven to us.[5]

It is impossible to live out the implications of my identity without the daily provision of God's limitless grace, poured into my life by his Spirit.

## Worship that transforms

This leads us back to the theme of this chapter – the worship of God. One of the first evidences of my being Spirit-filled will be that I begin to worship the true and living God.

Look again at Ephesians 5:19–20. Paul is describing worship according to the New Testament.

It flows from the heart. We are to sing and make music in our hearts. Worship is the overflow of a heart touched by grace. One of the great criticisms of Israel in the Old Testament was that their worship was elaborate, but their hearts were far from God. God is seeking those who will worship him in Spirit and truth – with sincere and surrendered hearts.

What is the evidence that my heart is right? The answer is that it will be filled with thankfulness, 'always giving thanks to God the Father for everything, in the name of our Lord Jesus Christ' (5:20). We are to cultivate a grateful heart and gives thanks in all circumstances. Thankfulness is fed by the memory of God's goodness to us:

Praise the LORD, my soul;
   all my inmost being, praise his holy name.
Praise the LORD, my soul,
   and forget not all his benefits –
(Psalm 103:1–2)

A Christian is a person who never ceases to be amazed at having been saved and blessed by God.

We express worship in song: 'sing and make music from your heart to the Lord' (Ephesians 5:19). Our singing is designed to declare God's praises. When we become Christians, we become singers. Most of us do not sing in any other context. Before I became a Christian, the only place where I ever sang was watching West Brom FC – and the songs were usually songs of deep lamentation. When I became a Christian, however, I became a singer. This was part of my new identity. Singing is the verbal and melodious declaration of our new identity. We sing because we have something worth singing about!

But notice that singing is directed to others as well as to God. We speak to one another in 'psalms, hymns, and songs from the Spirit' (5:19).

We should worship God in our personal devotions, but this should not be at the expense of corporate worship. As we have seen already, my identity can only be realized in the context of my relationships with my fellow Christians. We meet together for mutual encouragement (Hebrews 10:24–25). We admonish and teach one another as we worship together (Colossians 3:16). Paul refers to a whole range of musical genres. As we sing, we inspire and minister to one another.

When I look out on my congregation on a Sunday, I need to remind myself that many people are struggling. Someone has spoken of the miracle of the church car park. After a difficult week, we drag ourselves to church, feeling pretty disconsolate and downtrodden. But that won't do in church so, as we cross the car park, we set in place the fixed Christian grin that signals all is well. Why can't we learn to be honest about how we really are? When we sing, we are seeking to encourage one another and celebrate our identity in Christ.

For those who have lost sight of their hope, it is good to hear that 'in Christ alone our hope is found'.[6] For those who feel overwhelmed by sin and failure, it is a wonderful antidote to remind them that 'no condemnation now I dread, Jesus and all in him is mine'.[7] While for those in the valley of the shadow of death, how life-affirming it is to have the assurance that when we tread the verge of Jordan, we know that Christ will 'land us safe on Canaan's side'.[8]

When we sing, we affirm ourselves and one another in our God-given identity. I am a child of God. I am a new creation. I am free from condemnation. I am what he says I am, even if I don't feel it at this precise moment.

A life of worship leads to transformation.

## Another 'Oh wow!' moment

Before my wife Edrie became ill, we visited Niagara Falls. When we parked the car and turned off the engine, we could hear the roar of the falls even though we were some distance away. Sitting in the Maid of the Mist and feeling the spray on our faces, we were amazed at the power of the water surging around us. Over 3,000 tons of water flow over the falls every second. If I were to take a cup and place it under the relentless flood, it would fill and overflow constantly.

Every day, I bring my little life to the endless flow of God's grace and ask him to fill me afresh with his Spirit. It is possible to measure the volume of water flowing over Niagara Falls. But it is impossible to measure the infinite power and grace and glory of the Living God. These resources never run dry. His grace is without limit. He willingly and joyfully gives the Spirit to those who ask him.

As the Spirit moves in my heart, he evokes within me a desire to worship God. As I gaze at his glory, I am cleansed of my own self-obsession and transformed into the person I should be.

As a young Christian I discovered Philippians 1:21: 'For me to live is Christ, to die is gain.' Here is the heart of Christian discipleship. This is what the Spirit-filled life looks like. This is how we are to live out our new identity before a watching world.

### Questions
1 We become like the thing we worship. How does this work?
2 How does William Temple's definition help us understand the nature of worship?

3 Why is corporate worship important? How does it define us and how should it change us?

4 Begin to make a list of Christian songs that affirm our identity in Christ.

5 How do we maintain our relationship with the Holy Spirit? (Refer to Psalm 32:8–9; Colossians 3:16; Ephesians 4:31; Luke 11:1–13; John 7:37–39; 1 Timothy 4:2).

Part 3

# I AM A STRANGER AND A PILGRIM HERE

Christians are supposed to be fully engaged in this world, and separation from evil does not mean isolation from people. Our identity, however, will often cause us to clash with the surrounding culture. This is where life can become complicated and painful. Our identity is forged by the Bible and the character of Christ, not by the moulding of the world around us. I cannot become a people pleaser if I want to please Christ.

In this section, we will engage with issues that may well confront us if we try to model our identity on Christ. This is a major theme in Ephesians, because Paul is writing to Gentiles who have become Christians and who are now surrounded by an alien environment.

Ephesians sets our agenda, as we acknowledged earlier. This is particularly true in this third part of the book.

Our identity as Christians means that we will be out of step with many around us. So, how do we avoid the gravitational pull of the world? How do we work out our salvation with fear and trembling (see chapter 8)?

Most of us define our identity in terms of our relationships. What does the Bible teach about singleness and marriage (see chapter 9)?

Our identity brings us into conflict with Satan. Whether we like it or not, we have been called to engage in spiritual warfare. How does conflict forge our identity? How are we shaped by the spiritual weapons God has provided for us (see chapter 10)?

# 8

# Against the flow

## Ephesians 4:17–24

### Taken on trust

Terry Waite disappeared on 20 July 1987.

The son of a village policeman, Terry was the special envoy for the Archbishop of Canterbury, Robert Runcie. During the 1980s, he made a series of high-profile visits to Iran while attempting to secure the release of hostages. From 1985 onwards, he was involved in negotiations in Lebanon to try to ensure the liberation of four hostages, including the journalist John McCarthy. It was on one of those visits that he was kidnapped by associates of the militant group Hezbollah.

We prayed for Terry at church on a regular basis. Then came the welcome but astonishing news that he had been released. Terry walked free on 18 November 1991. He had been held captive for 1,763 days.

It later emerged that for most of the time of his captivity, he was kept in solitary confinement. He was chained to a radiator and blindfolded. He was often beaten and tortured. On occasions, his captors put him through a mock trial and acted out a grotesque mockery of an execution. The psychological suffering was as profound as the physical mistreatment. He described how he pushed away all thoughts of his family:

I found it too emotionally upsetting. I'd begin to speculate, and my imagination would run riot: are they well, has one of them died or fallen into deep illness? It was speculation because I had no information at all for all those years. So it was useless. Therefore, I said to myself, 'Keep away from that subject.'[1]

Imagine someone suggesting an experiment to Terry: 'We can arrange for you to return to exactly the same conditions that you experienced during your captivity. You will face the same uncertainty and suffering. It will be an interesting experience to reconstruct the misery of those years. Are you up for it?'

We could anticipate Terry's response to such a bizarre suggestion. No one in their right mind would contemplate returning to captivity. How could you? Why would you? It is foolish even to suggest it.

Sometimes, however, Christians make just such a foolish and inexplicable decision.

## Going back

By God's grace, we have been set free from the awful captivity of sin. We are new creations in Christ. The old has gone and the new has come. Our dreams and delights are different; our purposes and passions are brand new. Our feelings and our affections have been transformed. We see beauty in the face of Jesus Christ that we never saw before. We experience dazzling fellowship with God. We have a brand-new identity.

How could we ever go back? How could we be so stupid?

Well, that's just what we are sometimes tempted to do. Instead of remembering how grim and gruesome our former bondage to sin was, we look back through rose-tinted spectacles. We are like the people of Israel. In Egypt, they were living under the lash of their Egyptian taskmasters and experienced the targeted genocide of their sons. God set them free in order to give them a new identity. But, as they experienced the hardships of the journey to the land of promise, they lamented the loss of the luxuries of Egypt:

> The rabble with them began to crave other food, and again the Israelites started wailing and said, 'If only we had meat to eat! We remember the fish we ate in Egypt at no cost – also the cucumbers, melons, leeks, onions and garlic. But now we have lost our appetite; we never see anything but this manna!' (Numbers 11:4–6)

What a case of selective memory! They forgot the torture, the toil and the slaughter of their children. All they remembered were the cucumbers and garlic.

My new identity means that I have to live a new lifestyle, one consistent with being a child of God. As I begin to live like Jesus, the perfect man, I begin to understand what it is to be truly and fully human.

There is also a cost, however. I have to abandon my former identity and set aside my old way of living. Sometimes I forget how malignant it really was and I want to go back. It is the same as Israel returning to captivity. It is the same as if Terry Waite were to return to the chains and torture.

## Nonconformists

So, why am I so stupid?

Part of the reason is that I am still a work in progress. I have a new nature and a new identity, but I continue to battle against the old nature with its magnetic attraction to the old lifestyle. I am drawn back because of my longing for conformity. As a Christian, my new identity means that I make a decisive break with the past and seek to live in a different way. But how do I do this when I am surrounded by people who do not share my aspirations or goals.

I was once one with them.

Most of us want to be conformists. We are afraid of being seen to be different or being ridiculed for being 'peculiar'. Jesus was the ultimate nonconformist. He was accused of insanity and worse (Mark 3:21–30; John 7:20; 8:48). As a follower of Jesus, I have no choice in the matter – I have to be a non-conformist.

Paul addresses this issue in Ephesians 4:17–24.

The desire to conform continues to haunt us. Paul's strategy in combating this is twofold. First, he reminds the believers of the captivity from which they were released. Second, he describes the new lifestyle for which they have been set free.

# No longer Gentiles

Clashing with the world around us is painful and costly. It is sometimes tempting to give up and go back. Why not just fade into the background, chameleon-like? Surely the world wasn't that bad!

But this is selective memory. When the world around us seeks to absorb our attention and shape our identity, we need to remember what it was really like. Paul, therefore, begins by reminding them of the dark prison cell from which God has set them free:

> So I tell you this, and insist on it in the Lord, that you must no longer live as the Gentiles do, in the futility of their thinking. They are darkened in their understanding and separated from the life of God because of the ignorance that is in them due to the hardening of their hearts. Having lost all sensitivity, they have given themselves over to sensuality so as to indulge in every kind of impurity, and they are full of greed.
> (Ephesians 4:17–19)

Ephesus was a proud and sophisticated pagan city. We noted earlier that the temple of Diana was one of the wonders of the ancient world. But Ephesus was also a dark and godless place, stained with idolatry and immorality, and renowned for its addiction to the occult. Paul paints its spiritual condition in lurid terms.

We are not living in first-century Asia Minor, but this is an accurate and terrifying description of the world in rebellion against God, at any time and in any place.

It is marked out in three ways.

## Futile thinking (Ephesians 4:17)

The 'thinking' of the world is 'futile' – that is, it is vain, empty and pointless. The world offers satisfaction and happiness, but it cannot deliver these. All human endeavour is doomed to ultimate futility if it seeks to define itself without reference to the Creator.

Life lived without God is life lived in the realm of delusion. It is like a vapour or breath. Imagine looking from the plane window as it scuds across the top of the clouds. The clouds seem so solid and substantial. Couldn't I just leave the aircraft and dance across their surface? Don't try it – their solidity is an illusion! They will not take the weight of a human being and neither will anything in this world. Sex and pleasure, and work and learning are good things in themselves – how could they not be, since they come from the hand of a good God? But make them an end in themselves and it is like skipping across the clouds. Every attempt to think about the world that bypasses Christ will result in futility.

## Darkened understanding (Ephesians 4:18)

This futile thinking flows from a darkened understanding. Our minds are not neutral. Sin has warped our thinking, so that we look at the world in a particular way.

The evidence for God's existence is abundant. He is there and he is not silent. God has spoken clearly in a way that is universally understood. He has done this in both creation and the human conscience (Psalm 19:1–6; Romans 1:18–20). He is constantly bombarding us with the evidence of his existence. We just don't see it.

The problem lies in us: we are in the darkness. We are not victims of the darkness – we have chosen to dwell there, hardening our hearts and refusing to look at the light, with a blindness that is deliberate and wilful. In spite of all the evidence, we do not want to believe in the God of the Bible, because if such a God exists, we are responsible to him for all our actions. People supress this knowledge because they do not want to submit to their Creator (Romans 1:21–23).

## Reckless living (Ephesians 4:19)

Having cut themselves off from God, the Gentiles lost all moral restraints and lived to please themselves. They seared their consciences so that they lived lives stained by sensuality, impurity and greed. Sensuality involves throwing off all restraint and living according to the dictates of the senses. Impurity refers to anything in thought, word or deed that makes me unclean. Greed is a passion to possess.

Paul paints a devastating picture in order to quell our desire to go back.

Christ shed his blood to rescue us from this futility.

God shone the light of the truth into our hearts and drove away the darkness.

God has set us free from the dark prison of our sinfulness.

Do you really want to go back to this?

## In Christ's school

Having reminded the believers of what they have been saved *from*, Paul goes on to remind them of what they have been saved *for* (4:20–24):

> That, however, is not the way of life you learned when you heard about Christ and were taught in him in accordance with the truth that is in Jesus. You were taught, with regard to your former way of life, to put off your old self, which is being corrupted by its deceitful desires; to be made new in the attitude of your minds; and to put on the new self, created to be like God in true righteousness and holiness.

They have moved from prison to the school of Christ.

As disciples, they enlisted in Christ's school. Christ became both their teacher and their curriculum (Matthew 28:18–20). They were taught to understand their new identity. Everything that Paul has described in the first three chapters of this letter would have been at the centre of their studies. They would come to understand some of the treasures that were theirs in and through Christ. They had an entirely new identity, defined not by past achievement or present performance, but on the basis of grace alone.

Rescued from the prison cell of their former way of life, there could be no going back. Instead, they must now live a life that is different – and holy. Holiness is the single-minded, wholehearted and glad concentration of all that we are in the business of pleasing God.

We saw earlier that our hearts are a battleground. When I became a Christian, God gave me a new heart. At the deepest core of my being, I delight in God and want to love him and serve him. At the same time, I feel another tug, pulling me away towards my own self-centred desires and passions. In spite of my best efforts, it is an ever-present reality.

The longer I live as a Christian, the more I am aware of the battle that no one else sees: the battle for holiness, the crusade against lust, greed, sloth, envy, anger, bitterness and pride.

The process of working out the implications of our new identity is both negative and positive.

We must starve the old nature and feed the new nature; flee from sin and pursue righteousness; remove the filthy garments of sin; and replace them with new clean garments of righteousness.

It is the latter image that Paul uses here. The process he describes involves three distinct phases.

## Put off the old nature (Ephesians 4:22)

At conversion, we flung off the old way of life. We must continue to strip off the filthy clothes of the former identity. The old nature is dead, but it won't lie down. We must crucify it. The word that the Bible uses for this is 'mortification'. This sounds rather medieval – we picture musty cells in which half-starved monks try to beat their bodies into submission – but it is not what the Bible means. In a parallel passage, Paul spells it out:

> Put to death, therefore, whatever belongs to your earthly nature: sexual immorality, impurity, lust, evil desires and greed, which is idolatry. Because of these, the wrath of God is coming. You used to walk in these ways, in the life you once lived. But now you must also rid yourselves of all such things as these: anger, rage, malice, slander, and filthy language from your lips. Do not lie to each other, since you have taken off your old self with its practices.
> (Colossians 3:5–9)

It's so easy to flirt with sin. We just do not take it, or its consequences, seriously. We get near to the edge, thinking we can easily back away. But we need to declare war on sin, asking God to help us to resist its seductions. There is no room for compromise here. Jesus speaks about plucking out the eye and cutting off the hand that causes us to sin (Matthew 5:29–30).

We too need to be radical. If the films we watch, the websites we visit, the friendships we cultivate or the hobbies we pursue, feed the old nature with its sinful desires, then we must cut them out of our lives. This is certainly not a call for unhealthy abstention or a morbid asceticism. Rather, it is a call to identify the things that have an unhealthy influence on our Christian lives and refuse to allow them to control us.

A few years ago, I was speaking at a conference in Buckie on the beautiful Moray Firth coast of Scotland. During a free afternoon, a local fisherman took me out in his boat to catch some crabs. He had been a crab fisherman all his life and I was impressed by the way he hauled the crustaceans on board. I noticed, however, that he was very careful about how he picked them up and placed them in the basket. When I commented on this, he smiled and informed me:

> 'Of course, I'm careful. They are fierce wee creatures. They are fresh from the sea and angry with it. I've seen a crab catch hold of a man's hand and it won't let it go. I've seen it break a man's finger rather than let go.'
> 'So, what do you do if a crab does get hold of you?' I asked.
> 'The only way to break its grip is smash the crab against the side of the boat. If you don't kill it, it will hurt you.'

That sounds pretty radical, but it's exactly what Paul is warning us about in Colossians 3:5–7. If we don't break sin, it will break us. If we fail to take it seriously, then it will ruin our lives and mar our identity.[2]

## Be spiritually renewed (Ephesians 4:23)

Living out my new identity in my own strength and power is not difficult – it is impossible! But God has not left us to ourselves.

We have the power of God's Spirit to help us. If there is a gravity about sin, then the supernatural power of God defies gravity. The Spirit is a divine person with a sublime agenda. It is the agenda of transformation. He is actively at work, renewing us, to make us more like Jesus. The Spirit is the life of God in the soul of man. The power that raised Christ from the dead is transforming us. He imparts the power of life, a power stronger than death.

We must attend to our relationship with the Spirit, not grieving him by bitterness, or quenching him by unbelief. Our part is to come as empty vessels and to ask for his grace and power to be poured into our lives. When we come with our needs, we are not coming to a faltering trickle of water that may run out. As we have seen, we are approaching a Niagara of grace that can forgive every sin and give us power to overcome every indulgence.

The battle will rage for the rest of our lives, but it should be marked by ever-increasing victory.

## They must put on the new nature (Ephesians 4:24)

We were clothed in the righteousness of Christ when we first believed (Philippians 3:7–11). Now we must deliberately clothe ourselves in Christ.

What will this look like? Paul gives a helpful description when he lists the fruit of the Spirit (Galatians 5:22–23). The Holy Spirit supernaturally produces this fruit of Christlikeness in us. More than anything or anyone else, it is Christ who shapes our new identity.

We must not imagine, however, that the Spirit blesses spiritual inertia. The Bible is full of commands to work hard to co-operate with the Spirit in this process of sanctification.

- We are to offer our bodies as living sacrifices to God (Romans 12:1–2).
- We are to hate what is evil and cling to what is good (Romans 12:9).
- We must not sow to please the sinful nature, but instead sow to please the Spirit (Galatians 6:7–9).

- We must adopt the mind of Christ – thinking and behaving like him (Philippians 2:5).
- We are to work out our salvation with fear and trembling (Philippians 2:12–13).
- We must set our minds on things above (Colossians 3:1–2).
- We must put the old nature to death (Colossians 3:5).
- We are to clothe ourselves with compassion and love (Colossians 3:12–14).
- We are to live to please God (1 Thessalonians 4:1–3).
- We are to flee from evil and pursue righteousness (1 Timothy 6:11).
- We are to make our calling and election sure (2 Peter 1:10).

Putting on clean clothes involves deliberate activity.

We will need a daily intake of biblical truth. The children's chorus reminded us: 'Read your Bible, pray every day, if you want to grow . . .' We have to do this in order to meet with God and see Jesus in his Word. It is as we gaze at Christ, illuminated by the Holy Spirit, that we will begin to become like him. Reading the Bible clarifies my identity and self-understanding. It gives the Holy Spirit the opportunity to shape me in the likeness of Christ. It also reinforces my determination not to return to the world.

We will need to cultivate a healthy life of prayer. The Bible commands us to pray without ceasing (1 Thessalonians 5:17). In Psalm 27:4, David describes prayer as dwelling in God's presence, gazing on God's beauty and seeking God's help. It is not just working through a list of requests but having fellowship with God. Prayer can be hard work, but it is absolutely vital to spiritual health.

We will need the encouragement of the local church. Christian fellowship is the context in which Christian faith grows and reaches maturity. In the family of the church, I come to be shaped by common family values and am armed to go into the world and make Jesus visible, intelligible and desirable. We cannot survive for long without the regular fellowship we find among God's people.

# Alliteration

When I went to school, learning the rules of English grammar was still *de rigueur*. I remember sitting in an English class at the age of twelve and copying out page after page of notes from the blackboard on the difference between nouns and pronouns and those words that always had to begin with a capital letter. We graduated to clauses, subclauses and the like. Then we did alliteration, the repetition of identical initial consonant sounds in successive words – a device much loved by poets and preachers alike. The example given was lifted from the light opera, *The Mikado*. For some inexplicable reason I can still remember the 'dull, dark dock' and the approach of the executioner who would deliver his 'short, sharp shock'.[3]

That was once an apt description of our condition too: prisoners awaiting execution. But Jesus has set us free. From time to time, we forget what it was like and we feel the pull of the world. No one wants to be a nonconformist, if it can be avoided, but as a Christian, my new identity makes conformity impossible.

It may be difficult to go forward – but it is impossible to go back.

## Questions

1 Why do we find sin so attractive? Why are we drawn back to our former lifestyle?
2 Look again at Paul's description of pagan Ephesus. How does this apply to the world in which we live?
3 Avoiding sin means staying away from the edge. What does this mean for you?
4 Work through the list of commands given above. What do they reveal about the nature of the Christian life and the road to working out our new identity?
5 What should I feel when I look around at a lost world? What should I do?

# 9

# The home: men and women

## Ephesians 5:21–33

### He died during the sermon

I am writing this after celebrating my fortieth wedding anniversary.

Edrie and I grew up in the same church and courted for five years before we married. I loved my wife long before I ever asked her to go out with me. I can barely remember a day when she has not been the love of my life. But neither of us is blind to the fact that we have more time behind us than ahead of us.

The plan is for me to die at ninety-five, just as I have finished preaching a major sermon on a minor prophet. Edrie will be sitting in the pew and when the stewards come to inform her of my passing, they will discover that she too has died, somewhere between the last point of the sermon and the benediction.

That's the plan, but we are not optimistic about it!

It is more likely that one of us will be left alone, perhaps for some considerable time. At the moment, my identity is shaped by my relationship with my wife. It trumps almost everything else about me. If Edrie goes first, then I will become a widower – in one moment my identity will have changed.

Or will it? Yes and no. Of course, life will be different from what it was, but I am still a child of God, a new creation and a sinner saved by grace. If my marriage is the foundation of my identity, then I will be personally shattered. But if the foundation of my identity is in my unchanging relationship with Christ, then the rain may come down and the floods may come up, yet the house of my identity will stand firm.

Most of us define our identity in terms of our relationships. A relational God has created us in such a way that relationships are essential to our well-being. I am a son or daughter, a brother or sister, a husband or wife, a friend or colleague and so on. This is both inevitable and healthy, but there is a danger. Every human relationship is temporary. Some people long to get married, yet somehow it never happens. Others go through the trauma of betrayal and a painful divorce, while almost every relationship ends with the death of one partner.

In this chapter, we are going to explore the way in which the Bible approaches singleness and marriage. These obviously have massive implications for our self-understanding and identity. But before we go any further, we will look briefly at the tricky subject of gender and the danger of stereotypes.

## 'Male and female he created them'

Genesis 1:26–28 is the obvious place to begin:

> Then God said, 'Let us make mankind in our image, in our likeness, so that they may rule over the fish in the sea and the birds in the sky, over the livestock and all the wild animals, and over all the creatures that move along the ground.'
>
> So God created mankind in his own image,
> in the image of God he created them;
> male and female he created them.
>
> God blessed them and said to them, 'Be fruitful and increase in number; fill the earth and subdue it. Rule over the fish in the sea and the birds in the sky and over every living creature that moves on the ground.'

Human beings represented the climax of God's creation. They were given dominion over the world God had made. They were blessed and instructed to multiply and spread throughout the earth, and to begin to domesticate the natural world. The ultimate goal was the establishment of mankind's rule over creation as God's vice-regents.

Humans were created as male and female because only together could they reflect the image of God. They complemented each other and their difference was of fundamental significance to their God-given task of being fruitful and multiplying. The first command was to have sex. Yes, God is for sex, but sex is for marriage and marriage is for life.

Genesis 2:4–25 is a recapitulation of Genesis 1. Sexual union is blessed by God. Marriage is a solemn and lasting covenant between one man and one woman, for life.

In Genesis 3, the created order is disrupted. Disorder, death and sin come into the world. God promises, however, to bring salvation through the offspring of the woman (Genesis 3:15). The Saviour will come from within the human race – he will be formed from flesh in the womb of a woman (John 1:14).

The foundations laid in Genesis 1 – 3 are assumed throughout the rest of the Bible (1 Corinthians 11:3–16; 1 Timothy 2:8–15). The difference between the sexes is fundamental. Humanity has two distinct kinds: male and female. The differences between men and women are not merely accidental or incidental, but integral to their purpose. Gender differences vary significantly from culture to culture, yet the presence of a distinction between men and women is universal.[1]

## Smashing stereotypes

I was born in the 1950s and grew up in a typical working-class home. My dad was away from home six days a week, working. Mum did a couple of menial jobs, but her domain was the home and her throne room the kitchen. She taught my sister to cook, but neither Dad nor I were allowed into the kitchen. When I went to university at eighteen, I had to learn how to make a cup of instant coffee. My mum was a feisty and strong woman, never afraid to articulate her views, and all the men in the family treated her with respect and deference. She had very clear ideas about gender roles and these did not include teaching her son how to cook!

I married a feisty and strong woman who saw the world in a rather different way. The moment our sons were old enough, Edrie began to pass on her culinary skills. Most Saturday afternoons, they would experiment in the kitchen. When they discovered the wonders of food colouring, we were treated to green gravy and purple soup. Both of them developed a passion for cookery and continue to be excellent practitioners today.

How we understand gender roles changes from one generation to another. When I teach teenagers, they are much more sensitive to this than I was at their age, and it is refreshing to see how many stereotypes have been smashed. We have to be very careful that we do not impose our cultural understanding of gender on the Bible.

The Bible does affirm the complementary role of men and women, but it never resorts to stereotypes. Indeed, it is quite remarkable in its positive affirmation of both genders. If you doubt this, then check out the ministry of Jesus. In a culture that often treated women with contempt, Jesus is countercultural. Some of the rabbis said that it was better to burn the law than teach it to a woman, but Jesus encouraged women to listen to his teaching (Luke 10:38–42). He never made snide or dismissive comments about women; instead he used women as examples in his parables (Luke 15:8–10). Women became the first heralds of his resurrection and formed an important part of the early church (Matthew 28:1–10; Acts 1:12–14). Sadly, the church has not always followed her master's example.

Paul affirms that in their experience of salvation, men and women are equal (Galatians 3:28). When we think about identity, there is nothing to distinguish between men and women in their spiritual status or the divine blessings they receive. They also have equivalent experiences of justification, adoption and assurance. Every Christian believer is a new creation in Christ, and there is no particular attribute or character trait that distinguishes men and women. The fruit of the Spirit (Galatians 5:22–23) is gender-free.

We now turn to singleness and marriage, since they have huge implications for our identity.

# The challenge of singleness

At any one time, almost a third of adults are living as single people. Some have never married; others have been widowed or divorced. Single people react to the challenges of singleness in a whole variety of ways. For some it is a profoundly painful subject – they cannot contemplate life without a partner. For others, it is frustrating, but they have adjusted to their situation and are upbeat about the advantages. Still others are immensely grateful that they are free from the trials of marriage. They have chosen to be single and are happy with their choice.

The Bible describes singleness as a gift from God (1 Corinthians 7:7). It should never be regarded as God's second best. Paul does not mean that some people have a particular ability to be happy in their singleness. Rather, he is referring to the state of singleness itself. If, at some point, a single person decides to marry, he or she is not rejecting God's gift. At this current moment, the single state is God's gift – enjoy the benefits that it brings. Trusting God means knowing that my current condition, whether single or married, is his gift for me and I am to receive it with thanksgiving.

The Bible also teaches that there are advantages to being single. Single people are spared the troubles that come with matrimony (1 Corinthians 7:28). Sometimes marriage is a place of wonderful joy. At other times, it is a place of anguish and heartbreak. No wonder Paul wants to spare single people from this! And there is more. Single people can devote themselves fully to God's work:

> I would like you to be free from concern. An unmarried man is concerned about the Lord's affairs – how he can please the Lord. But a married man is concerned about the affairs of this world – how he can please his wife – and his interests are divided. An unmarried woman or virgin is concerned about the Lord's affairs: her aim is to be devoted to the Lord in both body and spirit. But a married woman is concerned about the affairs of this world – how she can please her husband. I am saying this for your own good, not to restrict

you, but that you may live in a right way in undivided devotion to the Lord.
(1 Corinthians 7:32–35)

We know all too well that many Christian ministries depend on the contributions of single people.

This does not mean that it is easy to be single. The New Testament is positive about singleness, but marriage is still the norm. Singles may have to struggle with loneliness and sexual temptation. It is when we feel most alone and isolated that we experience the most seductive temptation.

As Christians, we do not need to be alone, however.

The church should be a place where we are part of a family (Matthew 12:48–50). Here we find brothers and sisters, fathers and mothers and children (Matthew 19:29–30). Paul chose to live a single life and he was content with his choice. However, he had strong and abiding relationships that sustained him in the challenges of that life (2 Timothy 4:9–13).

## Marriage

We now turn to Ephesians 5:21–33, where Paul deals with the subject of marriage.

Paul challenges Christians to live a Spirit-filled life. One of the clear marks is mutual submission (5:21). It is in this context that Paul deals with Christians living in the home.

Let's begin at the end of the passage: 'For this reason a man will leave his father and mother and be united to his wife, and the two will become one flesh' (5:31).

Here is God's blueprint for marriage. It is not a human invention, but a divine revelation (Genesis 2:24). Marriage is God's idea.

Paul tells us three truths about marriage as God designed it:

### The primary relationship

Marriage involves a formal, legal and binding agreement before witnesses. A man leaves home and sets up a new family unit with his wife. Other relationships will continue to be important. We should honour our parents (Exodus 20:12; Ephesians 6:2) and we are to engage in a network of relationships throughout our lives. The moment we marry, however, this relationship becomes the primary one. This is why there is a command to leave. There is a definite break. It may be geographical; it must be emotional. From this moment onwards, my responsibility is to please my partner. I still love and respect my parents and, if I am wise, listen to their advice. But I am to put the desires and needs of my partner ahead of theirs.

The same applies if we have children. In an unsatisfactory marriage it is tempting to find the emotional intimacy and support we need from our children. This is a huge mistake. The best thing that a dad can do for his children is to love and respect their mum! Children then grow up under the secure umbrella of this love. We give our children roots and wings: they are rooted in the security of the home, but we are preparing them for the time when they leave the nest and form their own healthy relationships.

## A permanent relationship

The two are joined for life. The biblical pattern involves a commitment to a lifelong relationship: 'till death us do part'. This does not mean that there are no biblical grounds for divorce and remarriage, but the Creator's intention is that marriage should be entered into with the full expectation that this will be my partner for the rest of my life.

Every marriage faces trials and challenges – what would you expect when two sinners come together in close proximity and there is nowhere to hide? Marriage is not like a piece of sculpture you can leave for a month, only to return and find it unchanged. Ignore your marriage for a month and you will grow apart, fractures will appear. Marriage is more like a garden that needs constant care and attention. But don't be put off. Marriage is a wonderful blessing – one of the many good gifts that God gives his children. The key for the Christian is to trust God's grace and then work hard. Choose your love, then love your choice.

## A physical relationship

The two become one flesh. The marriage should be consummated and sex between husband and wife is one of God's gifts. The Bible celebrates this wonderful gift and instructs married couples not to neglect it (1 Corinthians 7:3–5; Hebrews 13:4). Sexual intimacy in a marriage is like the oil in an engine, enabling it to run smoothly. It may be a simplification, but if this area of the relationship is healthy and happy, then it is a good indication that the whole relationship will be healthy and happy.

Sex is a wonderful gift, but it is also a dangerous gift. When I give myself to another person at this most intimate level, I am making a promise. I am saying to this person, 'I give myself to you exclusively and permanently. I am committed to you in a unique way.' When I give my body, I give myself. My body is making a promise. This shame-free intimacy (Genesis 2:25) is a unique ingredient to marriage. Outside of marriage, sexual intimacy releases forces that are dangerous and destructive to our true identity.

# Wives and husbands

In their fundamental identity as Christians, men and women are identical. However, Paul makes a distinction between their roles, particularly in marriage:

> Wives submit yourselves to your own husbands as you do to the Lord. For the husband is the head of the wife as Christ is the head of the church, his body, of which he is the Saviour. Now as the church submits to Christ, so also wives should submit to their husbands in everything.
>
> Husbands love your wives, just as Christ loved the church and gave himself up for her to make her holy, cleansing her by the washing with water through the word, and to present her to himself as a radiant church, without stain or wrinkle or any other blemish, but holy and blameless. In this same way, husbands ought to love their wives as their own bodies. He who loves his wife loves himself. After all, no one ever hated

their own body, but they feed and care for their body, just as Christ does the church — for we are members of his body. 'For this reason a man will leave his father and mother and be united to his wife, and the two will become one flesh.' This is a profound mystery – but I am talking about Christ and the church. However, each one of you also must love his wife as he loves himself, and the wife must respect her husband. (Ephesians 5:22–33)

It is at this point that the Bible appears to be most at odds with our culture.

The wife is to honour her husband and submit to him. She is to affirm, receive and nurture his loving leadership (5:22–24).

This needs some clarification, for it does not mean that a wife becomes the unthinking servant to her husband. She is not a dormant doormat. Indeed, marriage involves mutual submission. Moreover, a wise husband will recognize and affirm his wife's strengths and encourage her talents. We need to smash stereotypes – she may well be a better driver or car mechanic than her husband. He may have better culinary skills. Only a fool would fail to delight in his wife's gifts and graces. Think of the picture of the wife of noble character in Proverbs 31:10–31: energetic, enthusiastic and enterprising. Let's face it, most decisions will be joint decisions and a wise husband will respect his wife's wisdom and insights.

It is not an unconditional submission – the wife's first calling is to obey God. If a husband wants his wife to sin, she must obey God rather than him, never surrendering her conscience.

Aside from all these qualifications, Paul is still quite adamant that the role of the wife does involve the affirmation of her husband's loving leadership in the home.

The husband must be willing to provide this loving leadership, sacrificing his own pleasures and desires to promote his wife's wellbeing (5:25–28). He is responsible for leading, providing for and protecting his wife.

Husbands tend to err in one of two directions.

Some just refuse to lead. Perhaps they have never understood the biblical pattern and have allowed the culture to shape them rather than Scripture. Or maybe they are just unwilling to shoulder responsibility. However, it is evident from God's perspective that husbands are responsible for creating the direction of the home. Of course, husband and wife will plan this together, but in the end the buck stops with the man. When Adam and Eve sinned, God called the man first and demanded an explanation from him (Genesis 3:8–12). To some extent, the fall into sin was the result of role reversal – the woman led the man, rather than vice versa. But the man bore more responsibility because he was supposed to lead and protect his wife. This means that the husband takes responsibility for the spiritual atmosphere of the home. Often, wives are frustrated because a husband will not initiate prayer or give the clear spiritual leadership that they crave.

Then there is the opposite extreme. Some husbands turn the leadership teaching into justification for a kind of dictatorial and controlling tyranny. They become harsh and use texts like Ephesians 5 to beat their wives into submission. They are making an even more serious error than the irresponsible wimpy husband, neglecting the command that husbands should love their wives as Christ loved the church. How was his love measured? By a life of sacrificial service that culminated in the willing surrender of his life for her good. This love is unconditional and purposeful. Christ died to make the church his holy radiant bride. The husband's goal is to enable his wife to realize her full potential.

To drive it home, Paul insists that the husband must treat his wife as he would treat his own body – nourishing and cherishing it (5:28–29). Now, 'cherish' is a beautiful word. The original Greek word carries the idea of imparting warmth and tenderness. We are reminded of the words of Matthew Henry:

The woman was made of a rib out of the side of Adam; not made out of his head to rule over him, nor out of his feet to be trampled upon by him, but out of his side to be equal with him, under his arm to be protected, and near his heart to be beloved.[2]

A husband's model is Christ and his motive is obedience to God. When his wife is happy, he will be happy too (5:28–30).

In the end, we may summarize this section with two questions.

- Wife, do you love your husband enough to live for him?
- Husband, do you love your wife enough to die for her?

# A profound mystery

Paul is concerned to encourage godly marriages and homes. However, Christ's relationship with his church is in fact the primary theme. It is not that Paul is using Christ's love for the church as an appropriate but random model for marriage. God's plans to provide a bride for his Son predate the creation of marriage in the garden of Eden. In this way, marriage is an illustration of Christ and the church, rather than the other way around.

Christ died for me as an individual (Galatians 2:20). However, the emphasis in the New Testament is more commonly on the fact that Christ died for the church. Christ loved his church in eternity. She was the gift that the Father promised the Son before the foundation of the world.

'From heaven he came and sought her to be his holy bride, with his life blood he bought her and for her life he died.'[3]

His love was sacrificial. He gave himself up for the church. He did not see any beauty in her, but he was driven by sacrificial love. For her, he suffered humiliation, torture and death. More than that, he experienced the wrath of a sin-hating God poured on him in the darkness of Calvary.

His love was intentional. His aim was always to make the church holy and pure. His bride must be pure in life, truth and love.

His love was victorious. One day, the church will be perfect and radiant, like a bride on her wedding day. The evidence of the New Testament letters shows that the church is far from perfect. It is easy to see her many imperfections. However, we must not dismiss the church – it is precious to Jesus and you cannot love him without loving his bride.

In this world, every relationship is transitory. Whatever our marital status, we cannot make any other person the ultimate foundation of our identity. Only a relationship with Christ will endure. This supersedes gender, marriage and singleness. Neither singleness nor marriage is permanent (Mark 12:25). One day, Jesus the bridegroom will return for his bride. When that happens, all pain will be gone – the pain of a difficult marriage, a shattering bereavement, an agonizing divorce or an unwelcome singleness.

Whatever our marital status, we should keep our focus on that day and allow it to shape our true identity.

## Questions

1 In what ways do we make relationships the foundation of our identity? Why is this dangerous?
2 How can single people support married people? How can married people support single people?
3 What does it mean for a wife to honour her husband and submit to him? How should this affect her identity?
4 What does it mean for a husband to provide loving leadership for his wife? How should this affect his identity?
5 How can we make our relationship with Christ the foundation of our identity?

# 10

# Fighting for what we are

## Ephesians 6:10–17

### The darkness of doubt

When I was seventeen, I experienced a crisis of faith that knocked the stuffing out of me. From the moment that I came to faith at eleven, I had a clear assurance of salvation and a deep joy in believing. I had the privilege of attending a church where the Bible was honoured and taught as the word of God. Each Sunday, my pastor would open the Bible, and we would hear God speaking to us. More than once, our pastor affirmed, 'This is God's Word. What the Bible says, God says.'

I had no problem in believing that, and with that belief came the knowledge of my identity in Christ. I delighted in Jesus and the benefits he brought. Someone gave me a copy of a series of sermons by David Martyn Lloyd-Jones[1] for my sixteenth birthday. He opened up Romans 3, and it was medicine for my soul. Like any adolescent boy, I struggled with guilt, but in Romans 3, Paul strips away our self-righteousness, brings us to the cross and shows us the fullness and sufficiency of God's grace:

> all have sinned and fall short of the glory of God, and all are justified freely by his grace through the redemption that came by Christ Jesus. God presented Christ as a sacrifice of atonement, through the shedding of his blood – to be received by faith.
> (Romans 3:23–25)

Jesus had paid for all my sins. All his righteousness had been put to my account. God saw me in Christ and nothing would ever change this. My heart soared! This is still one of my favourite books.

Then I began to study religious education at A level.

It seemed that everything I cherished was under attack. In particular, I was taught that the Bible might be a record of genuine encounters with God, but it was certainly not a book that you could implicitly trust. It 'contained' the word of God; it was not the Word of God. It was down to the individual interpreter to seek out the wheat hidden among the chaff. The reader became his own ultimate authority. I had to sift through the Bible and decide which bits were from God and which were not.

What are the implications of this? It is very simple. If I cannot be sure of the Bible, I cannot be confident of anything it says about me. Suddenly my whole identity is in crisis. 'Jesus loves me, this I know, for the *Bible* tells me so.' But does it and, if it does, can it be trusted?

I remember the crisis coming to a head one evening when Edrie and I were singing in a Christian musical called *Come Together*. Based on great Bible texts, it contained the truths that I loved. But the words stuck in my throat. If the Bible is not true, how can I be sure? How can I know anything? I was in a very dark place.

## Identity thief

Edrie, not yet my girlfriend, was concerned, and suggested that I went to see my pastor, Les Coley. Les listened to what I said, then opened his Bible at Genesis:

Now the snake was more crafty than any of the wild animals the LORD God had made. He said to the woman, 'Did God really say, "You must not eat from any tree in the garden"?'

The woman said to the snake, 'We may eat fruit from the trees in the garden, but God did say, "You must not eat fruit from the tree that is in the middle of the garden, and you must not touch it, or you will die."'

'You will not certainly die,' the snake said to the woman. 'For God knows that when you eat from it your eyes will be opened, and you will be like God, knowing good and evil. (Genesis 3:1–5)

'Who was the first person to doubt God's word and call God a liar?', Les asked me.

The answer is clear. First, the devil twists and distorts God's word, then he calls God a liar. His method is to attack the reliability of God's word. You cannot trust what God says.

Les prayed for me and gave me a couple of books to read. As we parted, he said, 'Remember, this is a spiritual battle. Put on your armour and stand firm!'

Gradually the darkness faded and my faith returned. There were more battles ahead as I went on to study theology at degree level, but for the moment all was well.

It is unhealthy and dangerous to suppress our doubts. Like pain, suffering and death, doubt is part and parcel of living in a fallen world. Only when we see Jesus will all doubt be gone for ever.

However, there is more going on than just an intellectual struggle. As Les pointed out, we are in a spiritual battle. The battleground is the mind, the target is the Bible and the aim is to destroy our confidence and shatter our identity.

Our identity is based on what God has done for us, founded on the solid rock of Jesus and his word. If I lose the Bible, I lose my identity. Satan is an identity thief. He comes to steal, kill and destroy (John 10:10).

## Know your enemy

In Ephesians, Paul describes the myriad blessings that God has poured into our lives. He reminds his readers that they will have to fight to keep what God has given them:

Finally, be strong in the Lord and in his mighty power. Put on the full armour of God, so that you can take your stand against

the devil's schemes. For our struggle is not against flesh and blood, but against the rulers, against the authorities, against the powers of this dark world and against the spiritual forces of evil in the heavenly realms.
(Ephesians 6:10–17)

I am a soldier on active service. I live in a war zone.

Christianity is not a walk in the park but is like living in the midst of a vicious and life-sapping battle against a foe filled with fury who will do everything in his power to destroy us.

We are opposed by a real enemy. We should not blame him for absolutely everything, but neither should we be naive. We do not just struggle 'against flesh and blood'. When persecution takes place or a Christian falls into serious sin, Satan is behind it. When we forget our identity as children of God and lapse into a new legalism, or a false teacher joins the church and poisons the spring of truth, Satan is at work. Behind all these things and a myriad more is a living, intelligent, resourceful, cunning and malicious foe.

There is an old Mack Sennett film in which a man is innocently stroking a cat. He turns away for a moment and the cat is replaced by a lion. The man continues, unaware of his proximity to a dangerous beast. Don't underestimate the devil and don't stroke the lion (1 Peter 5:8).

## Unrelenting malice

Satan hates God's people and will do all that he can to destroy us. Don't expect any mercy. He hates our service for Christ, our church, our marriage, our children and all our longings for holiness.

The largest seaborne invasion in history began on Tuesday 6 June 1944. D-Day was the Allied invasion of Normandy. After fierce fighting, the Allies gained a foothold. Nazi Germany was forced to fight on two fronts. Defeat became certain as they were crushed between two powerful foes.

Berlin surrendered on 8 May 1945, known today as Victory in Europe (VE) Day.

There were 336 days between D-Day and VE Day. These days saw some of the fiercest fighting in Europe during the whole of the Second World War. D-Day meant that the defeat of the Nazi forces was inevitable. But they refused to concede. Instead, they responded with renewed vigour and rage. Indeed, some of the worst atrocities of the war occurred during those 336 days. When rail transport was vital to ensure that troops could be moved from one place to another, it was often unavailable because the regime had other priorities. Train carriages that might have been used to transport soldiers were used instead for the movement of Jews to the death camps. In an act of unprecedented vindictiveness and viciousness the destruction of the so-called *Untermenschen*, or subhumans, was considered to be the most urgent priority of the day.

Can you think of anything more chilling than this?

Jesus Christ has dealt the death blow to Satan and all his malicious forces. In his life, he crushed Satan's head (Genesis 3:15 and Revelation 12:9). By his death, he disarmed the powers and authorities, and his resurrection sealed his victory (Colossians 2:15).

Satan is defeated.

But he refuses to give up.

In the brief period between the ascension and return of Christ – the period of time that the Bible calls the 'last days' (Hebrews 1:1–2), Satan uses all his malicious cunning to oppose God and destroy his church.

The book of Revelation refers to it in these terms:

Therefore rejoice, you heavens
    and you who dwell in them!
But woe to the earth and the sea,
    because the devil has gone down to you!
He is filled with fury,
    because he knows that his time is short.
(Revelation 12:12)

Satan is filled with a fury and ever-increasing malevolence.

This is one of the reasons why it is so difficult to be a Christian.

# Trust God and keep your powder dry

So how do we respond?

Three times in Ephesians 6:10–17, Paul tells us to stand firm (6:11, 13, 14). We do not need to go looking for the devil – he will come looking for us (1 Peter 5:8–9). There is no place for pacifists in this war, and eternal vigilance is the price of victory.

Behind our feeble efforts, however, there is the assurance that Christ, the captain of our salvation, is already victorious. The battles we fight may be fierce and bloody, but the outcome is assured because of what Jesus has done. We may lose the occasional skirmish, but the outcome of the war is certain.

God has made magnificent resources available to his soldiers. To describe these resources, Paul uses the extended metaphor of spiritual armour:

> Therefore put on the full armour of God, so that when the day of evil comes, you may be able to stand your ground, and after you have done everything, to stand. Stand firm then, with the belt of truth buckled around your waist, with the breastplate of righteousness in place, and with your feet fitted with the readiness that comes from the gospel of peace. In addition to all this, take up the shield of faith, with which you can extinguish all the flaming arrows of the evil one. Take the helmet of salvation and the sword of the Spirit, which is the word of God.
> (Ephesians 6:13–17)

Look at the images of armour that Paul uses.

## The belt of truth (Ephesians 6:14)

The belt was an invisible, but vital, piece of equipment. Soldiers often wore long robes. When preparing for battle, they had to tuck these robes into their belt. Without this belt, they would fall flat on their face. It is therefore a foundational piece of equipment, crucial to their success in battle.

The Bible gives us this foundation. Scripture shapes and stimulates the desires of our hearts by showing us Christ and causing our hearts to overflow with love for him. Satan, by contrast, is a liar and a manipulator of truth – the originator of fake news. He will tell us that we are mistaken about our identity and seek to win our hearts to his cause. We meet the devil's lies with the truth of Scripture. As we hide the Bible in our hearts, it gives us the strength we need to resist him (Psalm 119:11) and a sure foundation.

## The breastplate of righteousness (Ephesians 6:14)

The breastplate covered the thorax and abdomen, protecting the heart, lungs and intestines. Gladiators were trained to strike at these areas where their opponent was most vulnerable.

The heart is the driving force of our lives. It controls our mind, will, emotions, conscience and imagination. The devil can assault the heart with fear, anger or lust, and we need to protect it.

However, the principal way in which Satan, the 'Accuser', attacks the heart is with condemnation (Revelation 12:9–11). He whispers in our ear, 'How could God love a failure like you? How many times have you promised that you would not commit that sin? See, you have done it again! If everyone knew what you were really like, they would despise you – you should despise yourself.'

He loves to shred our self-image and to rob us of our identity as children of God. Once we believe his lies, it is easy to spiral down into self-loathing, despair and further sin. Or we set out on a new legalistic quest, trying to overcome the sense of failure with a series of man-made rules that we will never be able to sustain.

To defend ourselves against his accusations we need this breastplate. It is not our own self-righteousness – Paul once trusted in his own righteousness, but he came to see it as worth nothing (Philippians 3:1–7). This is no defence against the devil's condemnation. Instead, we need the imputed righteousness of Christ:

What is more, I consider everything a loss because of the surpassing worth of knowing Christ Jesus my Lord, for whose sake I have lost all things. I consider them garbage, that I may

gain Christ and be found in him, not having a righteousness of my own that comes from the law, but that which is through faith in Christ – the righteousness that comes from God on the basis of faith.
(Philippians 3:8–9)

When we trust Christ, God forgives all our sins. But he does more. He imputes the perfect righteousness of Christ to us and declares us righteous in his sight.

This is my identity. We struggle with sin every day and need forgiveness constantly, as we saw earlier, but our status does not change. We can come boldly to God and call him Father, because Christ has settled our debts and covered us with his righteousness.

## The boots of peace (Ephesians 6:15)

The Roman war-boot was a vital piece of kit, enabling soldiers to march and stand firm. In the midst of the battle, we need to be secure and stable, with our feet firmly planted (6:11, 13–14). Jesus is our peace (Ephesians 2:14), as described in Romans 5:1–2:

Therefore, since we have been justified through faith, we have peace with God through our Lord Jesus Christ, through whom we have gained access by faith into this grace in which we now stand. And we boast in the hope of the glory of God.

We have access to God's presence and a sure and certain hope. 'If God is for us, who can be against us' (Romans 8:31–39)? The stability that the gospel gives us will prevent us from slipping or sliding, retreating or falling back.

But we also need mobility so that we can proclaim this gospel to those who are in the grip of Satan (2 Corinthians 10:4–6). The Roman roads enabled the armies of Rome to march quickly from one end of the Empire to another. Our feet are to carry the gospel of peace to the nations.

As Scripture says, 'Anyone who believes in him will never be put to shame.' For there is no difference between Jew and Gentile – the same Lord is Lord of all and richly blesses all who call on him, for, 'Everyone who calls on the name of the Lord will be saved.'

How, then, can they call on the one they have not believed in? And how can they believe in the one of whom they have not heard? And how can they hear without someone preaching to them? And how can anyone preach unless they are sent? As it is written: 'How beautiful are the feet of those who bring good news!'
(Romans 10:11–15)

God has given us beautiful feet!

## The shield of faith (Ephesians 6:16)

The Roman shield was shaped like a small door and protected most of the body. It was made of wood and covered with hide or metal. Soldiers would interlock their shields, making themselves invincible.

The shield was particularly effective against the fiery darts/arrows that could kill and cause havoc. These darts symbolize the attacks of the 'evil one'. Satan's quiver includes temptation, condemnation, blasphemous thoughts, doubts and discouragements. Such attacks are often sudden, unexpected and destructive.

God has given the devil permission to attack us – he has access to our minds. It is very important to remember that it is not sinful to be tempted. Sometimes the vilest and most contemptible thoughts enter our heads. They seem utterly alien – and they are. At such times, we need to remember that Jesus was tempted. He was even tempted to worship Satan and so avoid the agony of Calvary. He was tempted but remained without sin. We must not confuse temptation to sin with the committing of sin. As Martin Luther observed, 'You cannot keep birds from flying over your head, but you can keep them from building a nest in your hair.'[2]

We defeat the devil's attacks with the shield of faith.

Faith is active. It is the deliberate decision on our part to trust God's promises rather than the lies of the devil. We believe that God will not allow us to be tempted beyond our ability to endure (1 Corinthians 10:13), and we reckon that the 'blessings' sin brings will be short-lived compared to the blessings of resistance and obedience (Hebrews 11:24–25). Faith is fuelled by Scripture and it flourishes in fellowship. Interlocked shields made the soldiers nearly invincible. We need one another – we are in this together (Hebrews 10:24–25).

## The helmet of salvation (Ephesians 6:17)

The helmet afforded vital protection for the head. Enemies used axes or broad swords to disable Roman soldiers by slicing their head. The helmet was usually made of leather strengthened with metal plates. This reminds us of the importance of the Christian mind. We are to be renewed by the transforming of our minds (Romans 12:1–2). Christianity is not brainless – we are to exercise our minds energetically (1 Peter 1:13). We neglect the mind at our peril. What enters our minds will determine our identity.

'Salvation' refers to the multidimensional blessings won for us by the captain of our salvation. We have been justified – the penalty has been paid and the necessary righteousness has been provided. We are being sanctified – God is at work transforming us into the likeness of Christ. We will also be glorified – made perfect in God's presence for all eternity. One day the battle will be over. We have a sure and certain anchor for our souls (Philippians 1:6; 1 Peter 1:3–5; Jude 24–25).

## The sword of the Spirit (Ephesians 6:17)

The Romans used a short, stabbing sword, about 24 inches (60 cm) long and sharpened on both sides. It was an ideal weapon for the close hand-to-hand fighting.

It is called the sword of the Spirit because the Holy Spirit was the one who forged it. Paul explains that it is the Word of God. It is authoritative and powerful, our principal offensive weapon.

We can trust it, because we can trust God.

Compare the temptation of Adam and Eve with that of Christ. As we saw earlier, our first parents sinned because they believed the devil's lies rather than God's truth (Genesis 3:1–7). Jesus, the last Adam, met temptation with the Word of God (Matthew 4:1–11). He chose to believe God's truth rather than the devil's lies.

Every day we, too, are faced with the same choice. Will I believe what God says about my identity and my destiny, or will I believe what Satan insinuates? The Scriptures contain all that God intends us to know in order to be saved and to live a life that pleases him. The Bible is unquestionably our most significant weapon in the battle with Satan. That is why Satan hates it. If he can make you doubt it, neglect it or misuse it, he is fully satisfied.

## Are you ready?

I was once waiting in the departure lounge of Atlanta Airport. Suddenly, I heard applause and noticed that all my fellow passengers were rising to their feet. At that moment, a group of US soldiers marched through the concourse. They were about to leave for active service. From the peace of the delightful peach orchards of Georgia, they were about to enter a war zone. The standing ovation represented the respect felt for these men and women who were putting their lives on the line.

We live our lives in a war zone. This should shape our identity and our self-understanding.

But we also live this side of D-Day. We are in Christ and we stand in his mighty power. This should give us confidence. We are to be victors, not victims; to soar, not sink; to overcome, not be overwhelmed.

### Questions

1 Do you think of yourself as a soldier? How does the metaphor help your self-understanding? How can it be misunderstood?

2 Satan hates God's Word. How do we avoid believing his lies?

3 We are to fill our minds with the gospel of salvation. Read Romans 5:1–5. What great truths concerning our identity are revealed here?

4 'The Bible is unquestionably the most significant weapon in the battle against Satan.' How do we use the Bible to defeat Satan?
5 Read Ephesians 6:18–20. How should prayer shape our identity as Christians?

Part 4

# I AM SHAPED BY
# WHAT I PRAY FOR

In this concluding part, we will explore two of Paul's great prayers recorded in Ephesians.

What did Paul passionately desire for these Christians? As we identify this, we will come to the heart of our identity as Christians.

We are people of hope. Our identity involves growth in our knowledge of God, the security of our hope and the transforming power of God's grace. The resurrection of Christ shapes our understanding of the future (see chapter 11).

We are more loved than we ever imagined. Paul prays that we may know that we are loved – this forms the foundation of our lives and strengthens us in trials. God wants us to know that we are loved with an unconditional and unquenchable love (see chapter 12).

Is our identity in Christ worth dying for? Paul would answer with a loud 'yes'. In these prayers, he gives us a tantalizing glimpse of the magnificence of our identity.

# 11

# People of hope

## Ephesians 1:15–23

### 'C'

Have you ever read a book that made you want to cry?

John Diamond was a journalist who wrote a regular column for *The Times*. He met his second wife, Nigella Lawson, while they were both writing for the *Sunday Times*. They married in 1992, shortly before his forty-fourth birthday. In 1997, he received a call from the doctor who had removed a lump from his neck: that lump was cancerous. Diamond had previously described himself as one of the world's great hypochondriacs. Now he had come face to face with his own mortality. He used his column in *The Times* to chronicle the course of his illness.

The column became a book – *C: Because cowards get cancer too*.[1] The book makes no attempt to portray Diamond as a brave or heroic figure. Nor is he driven by self-pity. He writes openly, honestly and with wit and warmth about his battle. After the removal of his tongue, he lost his taste buds and speech became difficult.

One day, in his car, he listens to a familiar radio programme. At first, he cannot place the voice that he hears. Then he realizes that he is listening to his own voice, recorded a year earlier. What strikes him is the difference between the man he is now and the man he was a year ago.

John and Nigella had two children. In the last few pages of his book, he describes how the family bought a dog. Why? For him, getting a dog was a happy occasion and it would leave happy memories when he was gone. Diamond had grown up in a secular Jewish home and was agnostic. He found no consolation in faith.

Buying a dog was his attempt to find some comfort in the face of death. He died on 2 March 2001.

## Eternity in our hearts

It is the incident with the dog that I find most poignant of all.

Human beings have an inbuilt sense of eternity. God has made everything beautiful in its time and has also set eternity in our hearts (Ecclesiastes 3:11). In every human soul, God has placed an awareness that there is something more than this fleeting and transient world. Life is like a vapour or a mist – we are here for a while and then we vanish (James 4:14). But we are meant for more. We instinctively know this. When I stood at my dad's open grave – he had died of cancer on the eve of his sixty-first birthday – I remember thinking, 'Even if I was not a Christian, I would know that this is not the end.'

That is why the story about the dog is so sad. It is a tragic attempt to deal with mortality but without any real sense of personal hope.

What has this got to do with my sense of identity?

Being human means that I am a creature designed for eternity. I am a creature so I depend on God for every breath in my body and every beat of my heart. But he has created me with eternal aspirations. Death was never part of the original design. I may try to suppress my sense of eternity, smother it with pleasure or muffle it with denial, but it is always there. The world around us shimmers with wonders that point us to eternity. When we hold a baby in our arms, or fall in love, or are moved by a sublime sonata, we are aware of an immensity that is beyond us and that one short life is too limited to experience anything other than its fringes.

Death is not natural. It has marred every one of us. It has also disfigured the creation. I dwell in a feeble body made of dust and I groan, knowing that there must be more:

We know that the whole creation has been groaning as in the pains of childbirth right up to the present time. Not only so,

but we ourselves, who have the first fruits of the Spirit, groan inwardly as we wait eagerly for our adoption to sonship, the redemption of our bodies.
(Romans 8:22–23)

I am also a person with hope. One day, our frustration will be overcome (Romans 8:19).

## Already and not yet

There is a real tension between the 'already' and the 'not yet'.

I am already a child of God. This is my true and abiding identity. I am loved by God and counted righteous in his sight, with the righteousness of Christ. I am set free from the downward pull of sin and brought into the glorious liberty of the children of God. I am ransomed, healed, restored and forgiven. The Spirit of the living God lives within me and grants me comfort, assurance and joy. I am joined to Christ. I have the assurance that he who began a good work in me will bring it to completion on the day of Jesus Christ. And there is so much more!

At the same time, as we've seen, I face a daily struggle against sin, and I need to repent and humbly seek forgiveness on a constant basis. I am an imperfect man, an imperfect husband and father, pastor and neighbour. Sometimes I can be mean, unkind and morose. There are times when I am full of doubts and my faith struggles. I often pray, 'I believe, help my unbelief.' When I get up in the morning, I discover aches and pains that I did not have before. I know that there are far more years of earthly life behind me than ahead of me.

Both these realizations are true and they are both ingredients in my identity.

So, how can I resolve the tension that they set up in my self-understanding?

The answer is hope. The most neglected of the great Christian virtues, hope is a vital component in my identity.

The first of two great prayers is the focus of this chapter. Paul prays here that the Christians in Ephesus may be people of hope.

Our culture associates hope with wishful thinking about the weather or the performance of a football team, but Paul has something much greater in mind.

He introduces the prayer by telling the believers that he has heard of their faith and love, and this has encouraged him to pray. His prayer is persistent and thankful. There is abundant evidence that God is at work here in Ephesus: 'For this reason, ever since I heard about your faith in the Lord Jesus and your love for all God's people, I have not stopped giving thanks for you, remembering you in my prayers (Ephesians 1:15–16).

## Knowing God better

What about the substance of the prayer?

It consists of three requests. The first is for a deeper knowledge of God: 'I keep asking that the God of our Lord Jesus Christ, the glorious Father, may give you the Spirit of wisdom and revelation, so that you may know him better' (Ephesians 1:17).

Humans were created to have fellowship with God. Remember how Adam walked with God in the cool of the day (Genesis 3:8). Sin had caused estrangement. Salvation involves the restoration of the relationship and the possibility of truly knowing God again. We cannot know God fully, but we can know him truly.

The greatest blessing as children of God is to know our Father. The prophet Jeremiah reminded the people of Israel of their high calling. They were made to know God and to make him known in a dark world. Instead, however, they had chosen to boast about other things. He, therefore, challenges them:

This is what the LORD says:

'Let not the wise boast of their wisdom
    or the strong boast of their strength
    or the rich boast of their riches,
but let the one who boasts boast about this:
    that they have the understanding to know me,

that I am the LORD, who exercises kindness,
    justice and righteousness on earth,
    for in these I delight,'

declares the LORD.
(Jeremiah 9:23–24)

If we boast about anything other than the knowledge of God, we
have missed our calling and misunderstood our true identity.

Throughout the Bible, it is clear that our greatest ambition should
be to grow in the knowledge of God.

Think of how the second book of the Psalms begins:

As the deer pants for streams of water,
    so my soul pants for you, my God.
My soul thirsts for God, for the living God.
    When can I go and meet with God?
(Psalm 42:1–2)

Or, again, think of Paul's personal ambition to know God better,
expressed in a letter that is roughly contemporary to his letter to the
Ephesians:

I want to know Christ – yes, to know the power of his resurrection and participation in his sufferings, becoming like him
in his death, and so, somehow, attaining to the resurrection
from the dead.
(Philippians 3:10–11)

Paul prays for the Ephesians, that their knowledge of God may
deepen. The prayer takes a Trinitarian shape. He asks the God and
Father of our Lord Jesus Christ to give them the Holy Spirit of
wisdom and revelation. God's Spirit reveals God to us. He does so
by opening our eyes to see Jesus, the image of the invisible God
(Colossians 1:15). The Spirit reveals Christ and, as we come to know
the Son, so we grow in our knowledge of the Father also.

John Calvin describes this as 'a firm and certain knowledge of God's benevolence toward us, founded upon the truth of the freely given promise of Christ, both revealed to our minds and sealed upon our hearts through the Holy Spirit'.[2]

## More to come

The great purpose of our life is to know God. But there is more to know than we can ever contemplate in one short lifetime.

Seeking religious freedom, 102 pilgrims set sail from England for the New World on board the *Mayflower* in September 1620. In late December, they landed at Plymouth Harbour, where they formed the first permanent settlement of Europeans in New England. They eagerly explored the narrow band of land on the Eastern seaboard of the American continent and were amazed at the new fauna and flora they discovered.

What they did not know was that before them lay a whole continent that would take many lifetimes to explore. They had no idea of the greatness of the soaring Rocky Mountains or the wide Mississippi. They had yet to encounter vast deserts, rolling planes or deep chasms, or thousands of other natural wonders from sea to shining sea. What about the glaciers of the North or a myriad of tiny islands in the Caribbean? Then, of course, there was the Gulf of Mexico, giving access to yet another land mass containing the Andes and the Amazon and the mysterious rainforests.

All they knew was the narrow band of earth that they were beginning to colonize.

When we become Christians, we are like explorers landing on a new continent. We are overwhelmed by what we discover, as each day some new vista of delight presents itself. We begin to try to plumb the depths of Scripture, only to find that we are merely paddling in the shallows. The knowledge of God delights us, but, at the same time, leaves us longing for more. We love what we find, but we are conscious that there is a whole lot out there to explore – an undiscovered country or continent. Perhaps it is true that in the whole of our lifetime, we do no more than discover the narrow strip we landed on. Even the greatest theologians and the godliest Christians have not progressed far in the divine science of the knowledge of God. We die, knowing instinctively that there is so much more of God to know. This is the principal goal of eternal life – to grow in the knowledge of God throughout the eternal ages.

The greatest joy of heaven will be to gaze on God's glory and spend eternity growing in our knowledge, love and adoration of God.

Revelation 7:15–17 pictures the pilgrim explorer after a long and painful journey, finding comfort and joy as he gazes on God:

Therefore,

'they are before the throne of God
    and serve him day and night in his temple;
and he who sits on the throne
    will shelter them with his presence.
"Never again will they hunger;
    never again will they thirst.
The sun will not beat down on them,"
    nor any scorching heat.
For the Lamb at the centre of the throne
    will be their shepherd;
"he will lead them to springs of living water."
    "And God will wipe away every tear from their eyes."'

The final chapter of Scripture also points us forward to a time when the intimacy of Eden is restored:

No longer will there be any curse. The throne of God and of the Lamb will be in the city, and his servants will serve him. They will see his face, and his name will be on their foreheads. There will be no more night. They will not need the light of a lamp or the light of the sun, for the Lord God will give them light. And they will reign for ever and ever.
(Revelation 22:3–5)

This leads naturally on to Paul's second request.

## Living hope

The second request is that the believers may have a fuller grasp of their hope and of the inheritance that God has prepared for them: 'I pray that the eyes of your heart may be enlightened in order that you may know the hope to which he has called you, the riches of his glorious inheritance in his holy people' (Ephesians 1:18).

In the Bible, 'hope' is shorthand for unconditional certainty. Paul prays for something that can only be accomplished by divine intervention.

The world is often a hopeless place. Even the most optimistic and upbeat among us will be faced with the inevitability of pain and suffering. To ignore the agony of a fallen world is the result of either a hard heart or a soft head.

But is hope no more than whistling in the face of the encroaching darkness? Aren't Christians just hiding from reality?

The answer is an emphatic 'no'. Of all people, Christians should take seriously the heartbreak of this world. But they also look beyond this world, to a future time when the curse is removed.

Our faith offers the hope of pardon, peace and glory to come. Hope is the anchor of the soul (Hebrews 6:19). It gives stability in the tsunami of life. It stretches beyond the storm-tossed vessel of our little life and anchors itself in solid ground.

> It will firmly hold in the straits of fear,
> When the breakers have told the reef is near;
> Though the tempest rave and the wild winds blow,
> Not an angry wave shall our bark o'erflow.[3]

Hope is future-orientated, enabling us to look far beyond the clouds that may be covering our lives at present. It gives us assurances that are firmly rooted in the unbreakable promises of God.

The writer to the Hebrews reminds us of the faith of the Old Testament believers. They lived and died, looking for a 'better country' – one that was clearly beyond anything they experienced on earth:

> All these people were still living by faith when they died. They did not receive the things promised; they only saw them and welcomed them from a distance, admitting that they were foreigners and strangers on earth. People who say such things show that they are looking for a country of their own. If they had been thinking of the country they had left, they would have had opportunity to return. Instead, they were longing for a better country – a heavenly one. Therefore God is not ashamed to be called their God, for he has prepared a city for them.
> (Hebrews 11:13–16)

Our citizenship is in heaven, and we are eagerly waiting for our hope to become a reality. We share this inheritance and the daily contemplation of it will shape our self-understanding and identity now.

> one thing I do: forgetting what is behind and straining towards what is ahead, I press on towards the goal to win the prize for which God has called me heavenwards in Christ Jesus.
> (Philippians 3:13–14)

But can we be certain? Paul addresses this in his third request.

## The power of God

Paul's last request is that the eyes of the believers' hearts might be opened so that they might know . . .

> his incomparably great power for us who believe. That power is the same as the mighty strength he exerted when he raised Christ from the dead and seated him at his right hand in the

heavenly realms, far above all rule and authority, power and dominion, and every name that is invoked, not only in the present age but also in the one to come. And God placed all things under his feet and appointed him to be head over everything for the church, which is his body, the fullness of him who fills everything in every way.
(Ephesians 1:19–23)

It's a living hope because Christ rose from the dead and secured it for us. The foundation of our hope is the historical fact of the bodily resurrection of Christ, not a parable or an illustration but a literal, physical, datable event in history.

It is an historical event, but it has cosmic implications. In this one event, God reversed the process of death itself. The whole cosmos will one day be put right, liberated from its current state of decay (Romans 8:20–23). Think of the *Titanic* heading for the iceberg and disaster. The whole cosmos is on a journey to decay and dissolution, but Jesus has single-handedly turned the ship around. The purpose of God is guaranteed. One day every memory of death and pain will be removed, and there will be a new heaven and a new earth.

This is confirmed by Christ's ascension (Ephesians 1:20). All powers and authorities are now at his command and he reigns over all things (1:20–22). Remember, Ephesus was a city steeped in witchcraft. Paul reminds its citizens that Jesus is Lord.

And we are in Christ, joined to him by faith, seated with him in the heavenly realms. His destiny is our destiny. His 'incomparably great power' demonstrated in these events is 'for us who believe'.

His lordship is exercised on behalf of the church (1:22–23), which is at the centre of all God's purposes. One day the scaffold of history will be removed and the church will be seen in all its glory. It will be demonstrated that in the cut and thrust of historical events, Jesus was ruling on her behalf.

This breeds certainty in our souls.

Peter begins his first letter with a bold statement, designed to encourage Christians going through fiery trials:

Praise be to the God and Father of our Lord Jesus Christ! In his great mercy he has given us new birth into a living hope through the resurrection of Jesus Christ from the dead, and into an inheritance that can never perish, spoil or fade. This inheritance is kept in heaven for you, who through faith are shielded by God's power until the coming of the salvation that is ready to be revealed in the last time.

(1 Peter 1:3–5)

God keeps our inheritance in heaven, and he keeps us through faith until we get there. What is our inheritance? It is God himself (Deuteronomy 10:9). Only God can eternally satisfy – he alone never perishes or spoils or fades.

In this way we come full circle. Our eternal destiny is to glorify God and enjoy him for ever.

We are like a child standing at the top of the stairs on Christmas Eve and peering down at the presents surrounding the tree. The best we can see in this life is a distant glimpse of the glories that are yet to be. In a world that desperately hungers for hope, Christians have hope stitched into their identity. It does not make us immune to grief and heartache, but it causes us to strain forward with confident assurance that one day all will be well. We know this because, through the sacrifice of Christ, God's wrath has been satisfied and we do not need to fear future judgment. We have been reconciled to God and 'it is well with our souls'.[4] Jesus is the only hope of the world – God calls us to shout this from the rooftops.

Don't we want our friends to share our hope too?

Barry became a Christian in his thirties. I had only been a pastor for a couple of years and the church was very small. Barry turned up one Sunday evening. The Christian message was new to him. He listened with amazement to the good news and within a few weeks had come to faith in Christ. I got to know him well.

A few years ago, Barry was diagnosed with cancer of the mouth, just like John Diamond. Edrie and I visited him in hospital the day before he died. By then, most of his tongue and much of his stomach had been removed. He was being fed through a tube and any other food and drink were forbidden. His speech was slow, painful and difficult to understand, but he wanted to assure us of his confidence in the face of death:

> I know I am almost home. I'm not afraid. Jesus is with me. They have told me that I will never taste anything again. But that's OK, because one day soon, I will be seated at the banqueting table of the king.

That is the difference hope makes. What am I? I am a child of hope.

## Questions

1 God has put eternity in our hearts. What does this mean? How should it affect the way we share the gospel with others?
2 How does the tension between the 'already' and the 'not yet' affect my identity and self-understanding?
3 Do you long for your knowledge of God to grow? How can we grow in this knowledge?
4 Why is hope a neglected virtue? How should hope shape our identity as Christians?
5 'The resurrection is an historical event, but it has cosmic implications.' What is the evidence that it is an historical event? What are the cosmic implications?

# 12

# More loved than we can ever imagine

## Ephesians 3:14–19

### Will God listen?

On the evening we learned that our grandson was severely disabled, I was due to drive to London.

Abe had been in hospital for several weeks and we had visited as often as we could. As time went on, it became more obvious that something was seriously wrong. Until the moment that my daughter phoned, however, we had no idea how serious it really was.

'It's as bad as it could be, Dad . . . ,' my daughter confided through floods of tears.

We arranged to visit the following evening, after my return from London, and so, after comforting Edrie, I set out on a journey that would take a couple of hours.

For the first half an hour, I was totally numb. I made no attempt to pray – I drove on automatic pilot. How could this be happening? How could this child, who had brought such joy, now be the source of such pain? When babies are born, you look at their tiny hands and imagine what they might become – a pianist, an artist or a surgeon. Before every child lies the vista of endless possibilities. But this little boy, with his golden hair, would never experience even the commonest joys that most of us take for granted. How would my daughter and her husband cope? Where was God in all this?

Only then did I think about prayer. My first train of thought was confused and negative. It went something like this:

I know prayer works. This situation is dire. Abe and his family desperately need God's help and prayer will bring his comfort and strength to them. But will God hear my prayers? Have I earned the right this week to have access into God's presence? Have I served God well this week? How have my daily devotions been? Is my life free from sin? Because these prayers are so important, have I earned the right to have God listen to me? What can I offer him by way of persuasion?

All these thoughts flashed through my mind as the car sped along the motorway.

## Legalists at heart

The confusion was probably down to my state of mind, but it was some time before it dawned on me how stupid I was being.

Clearly, the situation was dire. Of course, the prayers were important. But the assurance that God would hear me had nothing whatsoever to do with the state of my spirituality. Acceptance by God and the confidence that he was listening is based on his character and promises, not my performance: 'Therefore, since we have been justified through faith, we have peace with God through our Lord Jesus Christ, through whom we have gained access by faith into this grace in which we now stand' (Romans 5:1-2).

This is basic Christian truth. It is Christianity 101. How could I have forgotten something that I had preached and applied to the lives of others for forty years?

Yet, this is what we constantly do. At heart, all of us are legalists. The concept of grace is alien. We always want to earn God's favour in some way – to put him in our debt. We know that we are saved by grace alone, but then we imagine that the ongoing relationship with God is down to our ability to gain his favour by our good deeds and religious disciplines, conscientiously performed.

Legalism involves divorcing God's commands from their original context. God certainly cares about our obedience to his commandments and we should desire to please him. However, we have been saved and have become children of God. This is a grace-based relationship. It is out of our love for God that we gladly seek to obey him and do what pleases the heart of our Father.

Does that mean that sin does not matter? Of course not. When we sin and refuse to repent, the intimacy of the relationship is clouded. If we persist in stubborn rebellion, God will discipline us. But he will never cease to be my Father and he will never stop loving me. Legalism concentrates on obeying rules and forgets that grace has brought us near and will always keep us near.

The results of legalism vary according to our personalities.

For some, it leads to pride and self-justification. It is often accompanied by the construction of a set of man-made rules that cause us to feel good about ourselves and judgmental of others. Think of the Pharisees.

For others, it leads to a spiral of performance, failure, condemnation and despair.

The answer is to go back to the basic gospel principles and the assurance they give. With all my faults and failings, God is my Father and he will never stop loving me. I do not need to do anything to gain his smile – he sees me in Christ and loves me because of my position, not my performance.

I love my kids to bits (remember the rhubarb boys?). Nothing will ever stop me loving them. There is nothing they need to do to earn my attention and time. They have automatic access. When they were small, they might have disobeyed and issues had to be dealt with before the relationship could be restored, but I never put them on probation and I never threatened them with a termination of my love for them.

## Boundless love

What has this got to do with my identity? Everything!

Only as I grasp that God is my Father and that he loves me unconditionally and that he will never stop loving me, can I truly flourish as a Christian. If I doubt God's love, I will never enter into the fullness of joy that should mark out all God's children.[1]

This is exactly what Paul prays for:

> For this reason, I kneel before the Father, from whom every family in heaven and on earth derives its name. I pray that out of his glorious riches he may strengthen you with power through his Spirit in your inner being, so that Christ may dwell in your hearts through faith. And I pray that you, being rooted and established in love, may have power, together with all the Lord's holy people, to grasp how wide and long and high and deep is the love of Christ, and to know this love that surpasses knowledge – that you may be filled to the measure of all the fullness of God.
>
> (Ephesians 3:14–19)

This profound prayer can be summarized quite simply: God loves you more than you can imagine and he wants you to know it. There are many things Paul might have prayed for, but this is at the forefront of his mind. God really does want us to know that he loves us. He wants us to rejoice in it, bask in its warm glow and celebrate its boundless immensity. This is not self-indulgence, or an unnecessary luxury reserved for the elite of the elect.

## A sure beginning

Paul begins his prayer by reminding his hearers of who God is, and of the nature of their relationship with him.

He kneels before the Father, 'from whom every family in heaven and on earth derives its name'. God is the perfect Father. The concept of fatherhood is derived from the fatherhood of God. He was the Father of the Son throughout eternity. The moment we believe, we become sons and daughters of God.

There is a famous photograph of President John F. Kennedy taken at his desk in the Oval Office in 1963. Here is the most powerful man in the world in the middle of the Cold War. Then you notice something. Under the desk, close to his dad, is the three-year-old

JFK junior. He has an access not afforded to others, because of his unique relationship with his dad.

We enjoy the same access to our heavenly Father. On the one hand, he continues to uphold the universe and to move people and nations to their foreordained destiny. There is not one maverick molecule in the cosmos. On the other hand, he receives each of his children, comforting those who mourn and wiping away their tears.

Prayer is therefore a family exercise. Notice again that it involves the triune God. We kneel before the Father; we ask for the help of the Spirit; we long for the indwelling of the Son. C. S. Lewis reminds us of the wonder of prayer, in these words:

An ordinary simple Christian kneels down to say his prayers. He is trying to get into touch with God. But if he is a Christian, he knows that what is prompting him to pray is also God: God, so to speak, inside him. But he also knows that all his real knowledge of God comes through Christ, the Man who was God – that Christ is standing beside him, helping him to pray, praying for him. You see what is happening. God is the thing to which he is praying – the goal he is trying to reach. God is also the thing inside him which is pushing him on – the motive power. God is also the road or bridge along which he is being pushed to that goal. So that the whole threefold life of the three-personal Being is actually going on in that ordinary little bedroom where an ordinary man is saying his prayers. The man is being caught up into the higher kinds of life – what I called Zoe or spiritual life: he is being pulled into God, by God, while still remaining himself.[2]

## A solid foundation

Paul prays to the Father, that he might strengthen the believers by the Spirit so that they may be filled with the fullness of the Son (Ephesians 3:14–17). Paul's motive for his prayer is that they may be 'rooted and established in love' (1:17). He uses two images:

First, he wants their lives to resemble a tree with its roots sunk deeply into the refreshing soil of God's love. Picture a mighty oak tree or a majestic pine. It stands firmly, in spite of time and change. Its roots, most of which are unseen, give it stability and strength, health and fruitfulness. This is a common biblical image:

> But blessed is the one who trusts in the LORD,
>   whose confidence is in him.
> They will be like a tree planted by the water
>   that sends out its roots by the stream.
> It does not fear when heat comes;
>   its leaves are always green.
> It has no worries in a year of drought
>   and never fails to bear fruit.
> (Jeremiah 17:7–8)

The second picture is of a building established on solid foundations. The most important part of any man-made structure is the part you cannot see. The foundations give it support and solidity. If you want to build high, you have to go deep. We are reminded of Jesus' parable of the two builders (Matthew 7:24–27), one wise and one foolish.

Like a tree caught in a storm or wizened by drought, we face a thousand natural shocks. Like a building, we find ourselves rocked by the earthquake of adverse circumstances. When this happens, we need to know that our roots are deep and our foundations secure.

What is the soil in which we must be rooted, the foundation on which we must build? It is the love God has for his children. Our love for him is often fickle and vacillating. His love for us, by contrast, is constant and resolute. It is covenant love – a love based on unbreakable promises. It was demonstrated at Calvary and inscribed on our hearts by the Holy Spirit. God wants us to have a deep and solid assurance that he loves us unconditionally and will never cease to act for our good.

Life is painful. If we are to endure it joyfully, we must continue to trust that even in these circumstances, God has not stopped loving us. When we fail and feel useless and condemned, we need to remember that God will never turn away from us.

So often we are self-obsessed, trying to gauge and measure the tepid responses of our hearts. Of course, it is right to examine our hearts and, indeed, self-knowledge is a biblical imperative, but this can easily become unhealthy introspection. We need to focus on God's love, not ours. This is what Paul prays for. It offers stability and security.

## A staggering description

To help the believers in their contemplation, Paul struggles to describe this love. He wants them to 'have power, together with all the Lord's holy people, to grasp how wide and long and high and deep is the love of Christ, and to know this love that surpasses knowledge' (Ephesians 3:18–19).

He does not want them to have a superficial understanding, but to 'grasp' its greatness. The word he uses suggests a firm grip and deep insight, rather than a superficial acquaintance.

To capture their imagination, he raids the vocabulary of dimensional adjectives: God's love is wide and long and high and deep. He may be using these simply to indicate that this love is immeasurable. However, we are not pressing the text too far if we try to put flesh on the bones of Paul's description.

How wide is God's love? It crosses all barriers of time, history and space. It finds its resting place on every continent and in all cultures. It reaches out to all people, irrespective of race, sex, age or social standing. It calls into existence a multinational rainbow people of God. It is so wide that it can even encompass people like you and me!

How long is God's love? Before he created the world, the Father loved the Son with a boundless, limitless and eternal love. But there is more. In eternity, he set his love on us. We were chosen in Christ before the foundation of the world (Ephesians 1:4). He loved us long before we ever loved him.

How high is God's love? It is so high that it raises sinners up from the depth of their failure and sin and seats them with Christ in the heavenly realms. It blesses them with every spiritual blessing in Christ. They are welcomed to God's table.

How deep is this love? It is as deep as Calvary. The greatest distance in the universe is not from one end of the cosmos to another – it is the distance between the throne of heaven and the cross of Calvary. Without ceasing to be God, the Son of God took human nature, adopted the role of a servant and was obedient even to the point of death. And so that we don't miss the point, Paul adds that it was 'even the death of the cross' (Philippians 2:6–8). He was betrayed and beaten, despised and tortured, mocked and murdered. They hung him up like a carcass in the window of a butcher's shop. He stepped into the darkness of God's wrath, as he who knew no sin was made a sin offering for us (2 Corinthians 5:21). The first verse of Welsh pastor William Rees's best-known hymn focuses on this love:

Here is love, vast as the ocean,
Loving kindness as the flood,
When the Prince of Life, our Ransom,
Shed for us His precious blood.
Who His love will not remember?
Who can cease to sing His praise?
He can never be forgotten,
Throughout Heav'n's eternal days.[3]

Just so that we really get the point, Paul reminds us that when we have stretched every sinew of our minds and pushed our sanctified imagination to its limits, we have only just begun to touch the edges of this love, which 'surpasses knowledge'. It is wider than you thought, longer than you imagined, higher than you anticipated and deeper than you ever dreamed. You don't deserve it, but it is yours nonetheless, unconditionally and unreservedly. It isn't soft and it will chasten you if you sin, but it will never let you down, and it will never let you go.

## A stunning outcome

Paul now reaches the climax of his prayer.

As the believers begin to grasp this love that God has for them, they will be filled with the fullness of God. He has already prayed that Christ may dwell in their hearts (Ephesians 3:17). Later he will instruct them to be filled with the Holy Spirit (5:18). Here, he is thinking of the fullness of God the Father. Christians are joined to Christ by faith and indwelt by the Spirit in such a way that the life of the triune God is at work within them. This is realized and enjoyed as, by the power of the Spirit, we contemplate how much God loves us.

To be filled with his fullness is to be controlled by him as we surrender our lives without reserve or regret. It means to be transformed by him so that in every dimension of our lives we affirm his lordship and desire his will. It is to be satisfied with him in such a way that he drives out every idol and every other obsession, so that our hearts are filled with a passion for his glory above everything else.

Every day of our lives, we should be in a place where we bask in the unconditional, unquenchable, extravagant love that God has for us. This is no abstract theoretical subject. The New Testament always links the love of God with the cross of Christ. We start at the cross and we must return to it constantly. All our service is to be offered in the shadow of the cross. All our teaching must be an echo of the cross. All our living must be patterned on the cross. All our praying and living and suffering must be sanctified by the cross.

As we gaze at Calvary and consider his love for us, we will find a flame of love ignited on the cold altars of our hearts. We will learn to love Christ, to long for him and live for him.

## Overwhelmed by love

As I sped along the motorway to London, I came to my senses. How could I have been so stupid? Of course, my relationship with my heavenly Father is not performance-based. How could it ever be?

Perhaps the single most defining truth about my identity is that I am a child of God who can never be severed from my Father's love. Read Psalm 103 for yourself and you cannot fail to be struck by the intensity, intimacy and invincibility of God's love for his children.

> the LORD is compassionate and gracious,
>     slow to anger, abounding in love.
> He will not always accuse,
>     nor will he harbour his anger for ever;
> he does not treat us as our sins deserve
>     or repay us according to our iniquities.
> For as high as the heavens are above the earth,
>     so great is his love for those who fear him;
> as far as the east is from the west,
>     so far has he removed our transgressions from us.
> As a father has compassion on his children,
>     so the LORD has compassion on those who fear him;
> for he knows how we are formed,
>     he remembers that we are dust.
> The life of mortals is like grass,
>     they flourish like a flower of the field;
> the wind blows over it and it is gone,
>     and its place remembers it no more.
> But from everlasting to everlasting
>     the LORD's love is with those who fear him,
>     and his righteousness with their children's children –
> with those who keep his covenant
>     and remember to obey his precepts.
> (Psalm 103:8–18)

I have often preached on this psalm. Its words are indelibly imprinted on my mind. As I drove through the night, I began to feast on their riches. Here is medicine for the soul. Here is the key to understanding my identity:

'Jesus loves me, this I know, for the Bible tells me so.'[4]

It's a truth that is profoundly simple and simply profound. Did I really need to buy a book on identity to come to understand it? Why did I not state it and then just move on?

The answer was crystallized in my experience that night. It is the main reason why I wrote this book. All Christians know and affirm God's love for them. How could they not do so? It is patently obvious in the pages of Scripture. But do we really, truly believe it?

When we fail and fall into sin, do we believe it? When we face suffocating suffering, do we believe it? When the world mocks and derides our beliefs, do we believe it? When people reject us, do we believe it? When everything seems against us, do we believe it?

This is why we need to take time to understand who we are and contemplate the deep roots of our acceptance with God.

But doesn't all this talk about sin and unworthiness undermine my essential dignity? Of course, every human has an intrinsic dignity because we are made in the image of God. But, as we saw earlier, the Bible also tells me I am a sinner in rebellion against my Creator. He has not chosen to save me because I exhibit some kind of intrinsic worthiness, but because of his own character. Grace is love, given to those who don't deserve it – in fact, to those who actually deserve the opposite.

Christ died for us while we were still rebels. If my ongoing acceptance depends on my performance, then the basis of God's love is in me, not in him – and then I really am in trouble, for how can I be sure that I have done enough to guarantee his love? But if his love lies solely in himself, as it does, then I am secure.

The tree has firm roots. The building has a solid foundation.

Let's leave the last word to Paul, not from Ephesians this time, but from Romans:

You see, at just the right time, when we were still powerless, Christ died for the ungodly. Very rarely will anyone die for a righteous person, though for a good person someone might possibly dare to die. But God demonstrates his own love for us in this: while we were still sinners, Christ died for us.

Since we have now been justified by his blood, how much more shall we be saved from God's wrath through him! For if, while we were God's enemies, we were reconciled to him through the death of his Son, how much more, having been reconciled, shall we be saved through his life! Not only is this so, but we also boast in God through our Lord Jesus Christ, through whom we have now received reconciliation.
(Romans 5:9–11)

It is a love, and an identity, worth dying for.

## Questions

1 At heart, we are all legalists. Is this true? How does it manifest itself in our lives?
2 Why do we doubt God's love?
3 Read Romans 8:31–39. How does Paul help us to understand God's love in these verses?
4 'The single most defining truth about my identity is that I am a child of God.' Do you agree? Look through the extract from Psalm 103. What do we learn here about God's fatherly love?
5 What is the relationship between love, obedience and duty?

# Epilogue

Abe celebrated his first birthday a couple of weeks ago.

Of all the trials we have faced in our adult lives, this has felt like the worst one of all. Your kids are always your kids and you would do anything to protect them from pain, but sometimes you are powerless. I look at this little boy and grieve over all that he might have been.

But adversity breeds character and produces a harvest of unforeseen fruit.

As I look at the way my daughter and son-in-law care for their little boy with a fierce and unyielding love, I am overcome with pride. His two sisters, only a few years older than Abe, are intensely protective of their little brother. They call him 'the golden prince' – he still has a shock of blond hair! And as a couple we have experienced the kindness of so many gentle and generous-hearted people.

Having Abe at the heart of our family is a great blessing. The more I get to know him, the more I am convinced of his dignity and worth. I hold this little scrap of life in my arms and remember:

You have made them a little lower than the angels
and crowned them with glory and honour.
(Psalm 8:5)

God is bigger than any adversity we can face in this life. He is bigger than any heartbreak, bigger than lissencephaly.

And he is bigger than death.

Because Jesus conquered death, Abe too has a glorious destiny. This hope is more than mere sentimentality; I believe that it has solid biblical foundations and reflects the heart of God.[1]

I am persuaded that, one day, we will meet our grandson in the new creation and all the potentialities, unrealized in this life, will reach their magnificent fulfilment.

Brothers and sisters, we do not want you to be uninformed about those who sleep in death, so that you do not grieve like the rest of mankind, who have no hope. For we believe that Jesus died and rose again, and so we believe that God will bring with Jesus those who have fallen asleep in him. According to the Lord's word, we tell you that we who are still alive, who are left until the coming of the Lord, will certainly not precede those who have fallen asleep. For the Lord himself will come down from heaven, with a loud command, with the voice of the archangel and with the trumpet call of God, and the dead in Christ will rise first. After that, we who are still alive and are left will be caught up together with them in the clouds to meet the Lord in the air. And so we will be with the Lord for ever. Therefore encourage one another with these words.

(1 Thessalonians 4:13–18)

# Notes

## 1 Who am I?

1 Graham Beynon, *Mirror Mirror: Discover your true identity in Christ* (Nottingham: IVP, 2008), p. 16.

2 Richard Dawkins, *River out of Eden: A Darwinian view of life* (London: Weidenfeld & Nicolson, 2015), p. 133.

3 Albert Camus in 'Intuitions', written in October 1932, published in *Youthful Writings* (London: Random House, 1976).

4 I have engaged with the themes of Ecclesiastes in my book *Invest Your Disappointments: Going for growth* (London: IVP, 2018) pp. 33–45.

5 Charles Haddon Spurgeon was an influential nineteenth-century minister in London. Often referred to as the 'Prince of Preachers', his sermons were read all over the English-speaking world. This quote is taken from one of his sermons.

6 John Bunyan, *The Works of John Bunyan: Volumes 1–3*, edited by George Offor (Glasgow and London: Blackie & Son, 1856). See also Greg Gordon's blog (available online at: <https://regenerationandrepentance.wordpress.com/2013/12/10/sin>, accessed November 2019).

## Part 1 I am what God has made me

1 Richard Wurmbrand, *Tortured for Christ: The complete story* (London: Hodder & Stoughton, 2004).

2 Adapted from a sermon given by Richard Wurmbrand in the 1990s.

## 2 Undeservedly rescued

1 C. S. Lewis, *Surprised by Joy: The shape of my early life* (New York: Harvest Books, 1966), p. 115.

2 Lewis, *Surprised by Joy*, p. 266.

3 Lewis, *Surprised by Joy*, p. 260.

4 Robert Schuller, *Self-Esteem: The new reformation* (Waco, TX: Word Books, 1982), pp. 153–4.

5 J. C. Ryle, *Holiness: Its nature, hindrances, difficulties, and roots* (Apollo, PA: Ichthus Publications, 2017), p. 19.

6 J. I. Packer, *Knowing God* (London: Hodder & Stoughton, 2004), p. 151.

7 John Stott, *The Cross of Christ* (Leicester: IVP, 2006), p. 171.

8 John Stott, *The Message of Galatians* (London: IVP, 1968), p. 110.

9 R. M. M'Cheyne, *Sermons of Robert Murray M'Cheyne* (Edinburgh: Banner of Truth, 1961), pp. 47–9.

10 English poet and Anglican clergyman John Newton (1725–1807) wrote the words to the hymn 'Amazing Grace' in 1772.

## 3 Unbelievably blessed

1 John Stott, *Basic Christianity* (London: IVP, 1971), p. 135.

2 John Bunyan, *The Pilgrim's Progress* (Ware: Wordsworth Editions, 1996).

3 Lewis B. Smedes, *Shame and Grace: Healing the shame we don't deserve* (San Francisco, CA: HarperSanFrancisco, 1993), p. 5.

4 Dale Ralph Davis, *1 Samuel: Looking on the heart* (Fearn, Scotland: Christian Focus Publications, 2010), p. 102.

## 4 Unimaginably transformed

1 J. C. Ryle, *Holiness: Its nature, hindrances, difficulties and roots* (Darlington: Evangelical Press, 1979), p. 39.

2 From the sermon by John Stott at the Keswick Convention, 17 July 2007 (available online at: <http://authenticmission.blogspot.com>, accessed November 2019).

3 Kevin DeYoung, *The Hole in Our Holiness: Filling the gap between Gospel passion and the pursuit of godliness* (Wheaton, IL: Crossway Publishers, 2012) p. 47.

4 Paul Mallard, *Invest Your Suffering: Unexpected intimacy with a loving God* (Nottingham: IVP, 2013), p. 95.

5 From Clover Todman's sermon on John 10 (available online at: <www.widcombebaptistchurch.org/resources/sermon-downloads/?speaker=Clover+Todman&series=Johns+Gospel>, accessed November 2019).

6 Isaac Watts, 'When I survey the wondrous cross', in *Hymns and Spiritual Songs 1707–09* (London, 1707).

## Part 2 I am a part of a new community

## 5 Every barrier down

1 Paul Mallard, *Invest Your Suffering: Unexpected intimacy with a loving God* (Nottingham: IVP, 2013), p. 24.

2 John Stott, *The Message of Ephesians: God's new society* (Leicester: IVP, 1991), p. 123.

## 7 Everyone worships something

1 Rudolf Otto, *The Idea of the Holy* (Oxford: Oxford University Press, 1958), pp. 12–13.

2 Patrick Collinson, *The Elizabethan Puritan Movement* (Oxford: Clarendon Press, 1990), p. 356.

3 William Temple, *Readings in St. John's Gospel* (New York: Morehouse Publishing, 1985).

4 J. I. Packer, *Knowing God* (London: Hodder & Stoughton, 2004), p. 83.

5 C. H. Spurgeon, quoted in Charles E. Cowman and L. B. E. Cowman, *Streams in the Desert*, originally published in 1925 (this edition, Grand Rapids, MI: Zondervan, 1997).

6 From the hymn 'In Christ alone' by Stuart Townend and Keith Getty (Thankyou Music, Capitol CMG Publishing, 2002).

7 From the hymn 'And can it be that I should gain' by Charles Wesley, 1738.

8 From the hymn 'Guide me O Thou great Jehovah' by William Williams, 1745.

## Part 3 I am a stranger and a pilgrim here

## 8 Against the flow

1 From an interview with Terry Waite by Peter Stanford, *The Telegraph*, 3 September 2016 (available online at: <www.telegraph. co.uk/men/thinking-man/terry-waite-i-spent-five-years-as-a-

hostage-in-beirut---but-i-ne/>, accessed November 2019). See also: Terry Waite, *Taken on Trust* (London: Hodder & Stoughton, 2016).

2 You can find more on this subject in Paul Mallard, *Staying Fresh: Serving with joy* (Nottingham: IVP, 2015), chapters 6 and 7.

3 From W. S. Gilbert and A. Sullivan, *The Mikado*, 1885.

## 9 The home: men and women

1 You can find more on the subject of gender in the 'Further reading' section at the end of this book.

2 Matthew Henry, adapted from an original quote by Rachel Speght (available online at: <https://pages.uoregon.edu/dluebke/WesternCiv102/SpeghtMouzell1617.htm>, accessed November 2019). For Matthew Henry's commentary on Genesis 2, see: <www.biblestudytools.com>, accessed November 2019.

3 From the hymn 'The church's one foundation' by Samuel J. Stone, 1866.

## 10 Fighting for what we are

1 D. M. Lloyd-Jones, *Romans: An exposition of chapters 3:20 – 4:25: Atonement and justification* (Edinburgh: Banner of Truth, 1970).

2 Martin Luther, see: <http://theversesproject.com/verses/46/1-Corinthians-10.13>, accessed November 2019.

## Part 4 I am shaped by what I pray for

## 11 People of hope

1 John Diamond, *C: Because cowards get cancer too* (London: Vermilion, 1998).

2 John Calvin, *Institutes of the Christian Religion* (John T. McNeill, ed., Ford Lewis Battles, tr.), (Louisville, KY: Westminster John Knox Press, 1960), 3.2.7).

3 From 'Will your anchor hold', a hymn written by Priscilla Jane Owens in 1882.

4 Adapted from the hymn 'It is well with my soul' written by Horatio Spafford and Philip Bliss in 1873.

## 12 More loved than we can ever imagine

1 See also Paul Mallard, *Invest Your Suffering: Unexpected intimacy with a loving God* (Nottingham: IVP, 2013), pp. 180–96.

2 C. S. Lewis, *Mere Christianity* (London: HarperCollins, 2001), p. 63.

3 From 'Here is love, vast as the ocean', a hymn by William Rees (1802–83). See: <https://www.praise.org.uk/hymnauthor/rees-william/>, accessed November 2019.

4 From 'Jesus loves me', a hymn written *c.* 1860 by Anna Bartlett Warner (1827–1915).

## Epilogue

1 For more on the subject of hope for children who die in infancy, see the 'Further reading' section at the end of this book.

# Further reading

## Identity

Beynon, Graham, *Mirror Mirror: Discover your true identity in Christ* (Nottingham: IVP, 2008).

Hoekema, Anthony A., *Created in God's Image* (Grand Rapids, MI: Wm B. Eerdmans Publishing Co, 1996).

Ryken, Philip, *Grace Transforming* (Nottingham: IVP, 2012).

## Ephesians

Coekin, Richard, *Ephesians for You* (Epsom, Surrey: The Good Book Company, 2015).

Hughes, Kent R., *Ephesians: The mystery of the Body of Christ* (Wheaton, IL: Crossway, 2013).

Stott, John, *The Message of Ephesians: God's new society*, The Bible Speaks Today (London: IVP, 1991).

## Gender

Berry, Jonathan, with Woods, Rob, *Satisfaction Guaranteed: A future and a hope for same-sex attracted Christians* (London: IVP, 2016).

Roberts, Vaughan, *Transgender* (Epsom, Surrey: The Good Book Company, 2016).

Shaw, David, 'True to Form', *Primer*, Issue 03 (Epsom, Surrey: FIEC, The Good Book Company, 2016).

Shaw, Ed, *The Plausibility Problem: The church and same-sex attraction* (Nottingham: IVP, 2015).

## Hope for children who die in infancy

'10 things you should know about the salvation of those who die in infancy' (available online at: <https://www.samstorms.com>, accessed November 2019).

MacArthur, John F., *Safe in the Arms of God: Truth from heaven about the death of a child* (Nashville, TN: Thomas Nelson, 2003).